W9-AMW-595

2ND
EDITION

CHECKING FOR

UNDERSTANDING

ASCD MEMBER BOOK

Many ASCD members received this book as a
member benefit upon its initial release.

Learn more at: **www.ascd.org/memberbooks**

2ND EDITION

CHECKING FOR UNDERSTANDING

FORMATIVE ASSESSMENT TECHNIQUES FOR YOUR CLASSROOM

Douglas **FISHER** | Nancy **FREY**

ASCD | Alexandria, VA USA

1703 N. Beauregard St. • Alexandria, VA 22311-1714 USA
Phone: 800-933-2723 or 703-578-9600 • Fax: 703-575-5400
Website: www.ascd.org • E-mail: member@ascd.org
Author guidelines: www.ascd.org/write

Judy Seltz, *Executive Director;* Stefani Roth, *Publisher;* Genny Ostertag, *Acquisitions Editor;* Julie Houtz, *Director, Book Editing & Production;* Deborah Siegel, *Editor;* Lindsey Smith, *Graphic Designer;* Mike Kalyan, *Manager, Production Services;* Cynthia Stock, *Typesetter;* Andrea Wilson, *Production Specialist*

Copyright © 2014 ASCD. All rights reserved. It is illegal to reproduce copies of this work in print or electronic format (including reproductions displayed on a secure intranet or stored in a retrieval system or other electronic storage device from which copies can be made or displayed) without the prior written permission of the publisher. By purchasing only authorized electronic or print editions and not participating in or encouraging piracy of copyrighted materials, you support the rights of authors and publishers. Readers who wish to reproduce or republish excerpts of this work in print or electronic format may do so for a small fee by contacting the Copyright Clearance Center (CCC), 222 Rosewood Dr., Danvers, MA 01923, USA (phone: 978-750-8400; fax: 978-646-8600; web: www.copyright.com). To inquire about site licensing options or any other reuse, contact ASCD Permissions at www.ascd.org/permissions, or permissions@ascd.org, or 703-575-5749. For a list of vendors authorized to license ASCD e-books to institutions, see www.ascd.org/epubs. Send translation inquiries to translations@ascd.org.

Cover photo by Kevin Davis.

All referenced trademarks are the property of their respective owners.

All web links in this book are correct as of the publication date below but may have become inactive or otherwise modified since that time. If you notice a deactivated or changed link, please e-mail books@ascd.org with the words "Link Update" in the subject line. In your message, please specify the web link, the book title, and the page number on which the link appears.

PAPERBACK ISBN: 978-1-4166-1922-2   ASCD product #115011
Quantity discounts: 10–49, 10%; 50+, 15%; 1,000+, special discounts (e-mail programteam@ascd.org or call 800-933-2723, ext. 5773, or 703-575-5773). Also available in e-book formats. For desk copies, go to www.ascd.org/deskcopy.

ASCD Member Book No. FY15-3 (Dec. 2014, P). ASCD Member Books mail to Premium (P), Select (S), and Institutional Plus (I+) members on this schedule: Jan, PSI+; Feb, P; Apr, PSI+; May, P; Jul, PSI+; Aug, P; Sep, PSI+; Nov, PSI+; Dec, P. For current details on membership, see www.ascd.org/membership.

Library of Congress Cataloging-in-Publication Data

Fisher, Douglas, 1965–
    Checking for understanding : formative assessment techniques for your classroom /
Douglas Fisher and Nancy Frey. — Second edition.
        pages cm
    Includes bibliographical references and index.
    ISBN 978-1-4166-1922-2 (pbk. : alk. paper)
1. Classroom management. 2. Effective teaching. I. Frey, Nancy, 1959– II. Title.
    LB3013.F515 2014
    371.102'4—dc23
                                        2014023985

23 22 21 20 19 18 17 16 15 14   1 2 3 4 5 6 7 8 9 10 11 12

CHECKING FOR UNDERSTANDING

FORMATIVE ASSESSMENT TECHNIQUES FOR YOUR CLASSROOM

2ND EDITION

Preface

It's breathtaking (and a bit intimidating) to witness the changes in education in this century. The most obvious change, of course, is the role technology has assumed in classrooms. Where once we talked about enhancement, now we recognize that technology is an essential tool for communication and collaboration. Less apparent, at least on the surface, is the way in which data has become an essential element in any conversation about teaching and learning. Most schools have a data room to display information, and nearly every school is required to report these data annually to the community. And our profession's focus on post-secondary outcomes is causing all of us to consider what happens to our graduates after they leave high school.

But educators recognize that the devices in a classroom, the results on the state achievement test, and the college- and career-readiness standards can't equip them with the information they need to figure out what to do in the next five minutes. Only formative assessment practices can deliver timely data about what students understand. Without formative assessment data, teaching is aimed at the middle. We'll never know which students were ready for a stretch, and which needed reteaching. Unfortunately, too often formative assessment has been reduced to two or three district benchmark tests, with little attention given to the data that surround us every day.

Seeing the Data Each Day

Talented educators know that the opportunities for fine-grained analysis of student learning are all around us. Each time we host a discussion with students, examine a child's writing, or listen closely to a question, there's a chance to assess formatively. But these possibilities are wasted if there isn't intention. Wise teachers know that discussions, writing assignments, and such are not compliance checks. They are to teachers what paint is to an artist—the medium we work in. It's how we paint our own picture of the learning in front of us.

We have organized the book to highlight each of these media: oral and written language, questions, projects, and performances. We include tests as a formative assessment method because they can be used to inform future instruction if used intentionally. And finally, we discuss the need for common formative assessments and consensus scoring as a means for facilitating the thoughtful conversations among educators about student learning.

Much has changed in the field of formative assessment since the first edition of *Checking for Understanding* was published in 2007, and we have tried to incorporate these practices into this book. As technology has taken on greater importance, we see teachers use devices such as audience response systems to gather formative assessment data. In addition, we have revised the common formative assessment chapter to reflect the regular practice of teachers who gather to examine student data. As well, we have integrated newer instructional routines, such as the use of close reading and text-dependent questions, in order to better reflect newer approaches for developing college- and career-ready students.

The second edition of *Checking for Understanding* has given us the opportunity to contextualize this work within a Framework for Intentional and Targeted Teaching™. The practice of checking for understanding doesn't operate in isolation, but rather is an essential element for a gradual release of responsibility instructional framework. It is also a vital facet for providing feedback to students, and a means for gathering and analyzing data. Therefore, we have consolidated practices discussed in other ASCD publications, notably our work on guided instruction, formative assessment systems, data analysis, and quality instruction.

We are as excited as you are about the innovative practices we are witnessing in classrooms across the globe. As we move forward, our collective challenge is in keeping pace with change while retaining the time-honored practices that have served generations of learners so well. How will we know what practices should be pursued and what should be abandoned? By checking for understanding, of course!

1

Why Check for Understanding?

Checking for understanding permeates the teaching world. If you doubt that, consider the last lecture you heard. Whether the lecture was about chemical reactions, the great American novel, or the causes of World War II, the person speaking most likely checked for your understanding several times during the lecture by using such common prompts as "Any questions?", "Did you all get that?", "Everybody understand?", or "Does that make sense?"

Rather than respond to these questions, most learners will sit quietly, and the lecturer doesn't know whether they understand, they are too confused to answer, they think they get it (but are off base), or they are too embarrassed to show their lack of understanding in front of others. Such general questions are simply not sufficient in determining whether or not students "get it."

Additionally, students aren't always self-regulated learners. They may not be aware of what they do or do not understand. They sometimes think they get it, when they really don't. If you doubt this, consider how often you have heard students comment, "I thought I knew this stuff, but I bombed the exam."

Much of the checking for understanding done in schools is ineffective. Thankfully, there are a number of ways to address the situation. We've organized this book, and the ways that teachers can check for understanding, into larger categories, including oral language, questioning, writing, projects and performances, tests, and schoolwide approaches. In this chapter, we'll explore checking for understanding in terms of what it is, what it is not, and how it links to other teaching initiatives.

What Is Checking for Understanding?

Checking for understanding is an important step in the teaching and learning process. The background knowledge that students bring into the classroom influences how they understand the material you share and the lessons or learning opportunities you provide. Unless you check for understanding, it is difficult to know exactly what students are getting out of the lesson. In fact, checking for understanding is part of a formative assessment system in which teachers identify learning goals, provide students feedback, and then plan instruction based on students' errors and misconceptions. Although the focus of this book is on strategies for checking for understanding, it is important to know how these strategies are used to improve student achievement as part of a more comprehensive system. Hattie and Timperley (2007) identified these phases as feed-up, feedback, and feed-forward. Note that checking for understanding is an important link between feed-up and the feedback students receive as well as the future lessons teachers plan.

Feed-up: Clarifying the purpose. The first component of a comprehensive formative assessment system involves an established purpose, objective, or learning target. When students understand the goal of the instruction, they are more likely to focus on the learning tasks at hand. When the goal "is clear, when high commitment is secured for it, and when belief in eventual success is high," student effort is amplified and achievement increases (Kluger & DeNisi, 1996, p. 260). Having a purpose isn't new, but it is critical to the implementation of a formative assessment system because when teachers have a clear purpose, they can align their checking for understanding strategies with their intended outcomes. For example, when an established purpose relates to comparing and contrasting characteristics of insects and arthropods, students know what to expect in the lesson and the teacher can plan instructional events such as shared readings, collaborative learning, and investigations to ensure that students focus their attention on this content. Similarly, when the established purpose is to persuade a reader using argumentation and facts, the students have a clear sense of what is expected and the teacher can plan instruction. In sum, a clear purpose is a critical component of an effective feedback system.

Feedback: Responding to student work. The second component of a comprehensive formative assessment system, and the one that is more commonly recognized, relates to the individual responses to their work that students receive from teachers. Of course, these responses should be directly related to the purpose and performance goal. The best feedback provides students with information about their progress or success and what course of action they can take to improve their understanding to meet the expected standard (Brookhart, 2008). Ideally, feedback occurs as students complete tasks so that they can continue to master content. If learning is the goal, teachers should not limit feedback to a summative review but should rather provide formative feedback that students could use to improve their performance. For example, in a unit of study on writing high-quality introductions, Kelly Johnson provided her students multiple opportunities to introduce topics using various techniques such as humor, questions, startling statistic, direct quotation, and so on. For each introduction they produced, Dr. Johnson provided feedback using a rubric so that students could revise their introduction and use that information on their next attempt. She did not simply note the mechanical errors students made but rather acknowledged areas of success and provided recommendations for students to focus on in their next drafts.

Feed-forward: Modifying instruction. The final component required for creating a formative assessment system involves using data to plan instruction. Feed-forward systems involve greater flexibility in lesson planning, because teachers can't simply follow a script or implement a series of lesson plans that are written in stone. This is the formative aspect of checking for understanding and one that is often missing. When teachers examine student work, whether it is from a daily checking for understanding task or a common formative assessment tool, they can use that information to plan instruction and intervention. For example, students in a 3rd grade class completed a collaborative poster in response to a word problem. One of the groups had a problem that read: *Six students are sitting at each table in the lunchroom. There are 23 tables. How many students are in the lunchroom?* The students in this class knew that they had to answer the question using words, numbers, and pictures. Not only did the students with this problem do it wrong, but nearly every group had the wrong answer. Given this information, the teacher knew that she needed to provide more modeling for her students about how to solve word problems. The feed-forward, in this case, required a whole-class reteaching.

Alternatively, in a 5th grade classroom, the teacher noted that six students regularly capitalized random words in sentences. Mauricio, for example, had the words *fun*, *very*, *excited*, and *challenge* incorrectly capitalized in the first paragraph. Given that the rest of the class was not making this type of error, their teacher knew that feed-forward instruction with the whole class was not necessary. Instead, he needed to provide additional guided instruction for the students who consistently made this type of error.

Know the Difference Between a Mistake and an Error

All of us make mistakes. If we're fortunate, we catch ourselves (or someone else does) and we do our best to correct it. Typically mistakes occur due to a lack of attention. But importantly, once pointed out, there is immediate recognition and usually knowledge of the corrective action to take. Our students do this as well. They make mistakes due to fatigue, carelessness, or inattention, and as a result their performance suffers. However, they possess the knowledge and can avoid the mistake in the future by increasing their attention. It's easy for us to recognize mistakes by knowing the student's previous work. A mistake strikes us as being uncharacteristic, usually because we have seen the student do similar work correctly in past. Mistakes can be huge, and we aren't minimizing them. NASA lost a $125 million orbiter in 1999 because one engineering team used metric measures while another used English measures. That was a costly mistake, but it wasn't because the teams didn't know how to use the metric system. Had the mistake been caught in time, they would have known precisely how to correct it. Errors, on the other hand, occur because of a lack of knowledge. Even when alerted, the learner isn't quite sure what to do next. He lacks the skills or conceptual understanding to do anything differently when given another opportunity to try. Correcting mistakes while failing to address errors can be a costly waste of instructional time.

Errors fall into four broad categories and, when analyzed, can provide teachers with information they need to make instruction more precise. Some students make *factual errors* that interfere with their ability to perform with accuracy. Life sciences teacher Kenya Jackson sees this with her students who have difficulty correctly defining the differences and similarities between recessive and dominant traits. She also witnesses some of her students making *procedural errors* that make it difficult to apply factual information. "When I initially teach how to use a Punnett square to predict probability about genotype," she said, "they can tell me what dominate and recessive alleles are, but they can't calculate them in a meaningful way." A third type is a *transformation error*. Ms. Jackson notes that the Punnett square procedure is only valid when the traits are independent of one another. "Although I use examples and nonexamples in my teaching, some of them still overgeneralize the procedure and try to use it with polygenic traits such as hair color," she said. "For some, they have learned a tool and now they want to use it in every situation." A fourth type of error, the *misconception*, can result from the teaching itself. "I have to stay on guard for this," Ms. Jackson said. "Because I teach them Punnett squares, many of them hold this misconception that one gene is always responsible for one trait. These ideas can be stubbornly held, so I have to teach directly with misconceptions in mind."

An important part of the learning process is identifying and confronting misconceptions that can interfere with learning. Consider, for instance, how appreciating and addressing students' misconceptions can inform instruction in the following areas:

• Incorrect beliefs of young children that paintings are produced in factories (Wolf, 1987)
• Elementary students' misunderstanding that an equal sign in mathematics indicates an operation, rather than a relation (Ginsburg, 1982)
• K–3 students' beliefs that Native Americans who lived in tepees did so because they were poor and could not afford a house (Brophy & Alleman, 2002)
• Mistaken beliefs about living creatures—for example, that flies can walk on the ceiling because they have suction cups on their feet, and beavers use their tails as a trowel (Smith, 1920)
• Science students' misconception that larger objects are heavier than smaller ones (Schauble, 1996)
• The belief by adolescents (and adults) that there is a greater likelihood of "tails" in a coin toss after a series of "heads"—also known as the "Gambler's Fallacy" (Shaughnessy, 1977)

The act of checking for understanding not only identifies errors and misconceptions but also can improve learning. In a study by Vosniadou, Ioannides, Dimitrakopoulou, and Papademetriou (2001), two groups of students participated in a physics lesson. With one group of students, the researchers checked for understanding before moving on to the next part of the lesson. They did so by presenting students with a brief scenario and asking them to predict and explain the outcome. The other group participated in the exact same lesson, but without any pauses to check for understanding. As you might expect, the findings clearly demonstrated that the first group had a significantly greater increase in post-test over pre-test performance on assessments of content knowledge. In addition, short but frequent quizzes of newly learned information appear to increase students' retention and retrieval of information, including that which is related but not tested, and assists learners in better organizing information (Roediger, Putnam, & Smith, 2011).

Checking for understanding provides students with a model of good study skills. When their teachers regularly check for understanding, students become increasingly aware of how to monitor their own understanding. In the classic study by Bloom and Broder (1950), students performing well below grade level were paired with students who were successful. The successful students shared the variety of ways that they used to check that they understood the material. For example, the successful students restated sections of the material in their own words, asked themselves questions about the material, and thought of examples that related to the information they were reading. The students identified as at risk of school failure first observed and then began to incorporate these strategies into their own studying. Comprehension test scores soared. These findings held when the performance changes were compared with a control group who spent the same amount of time with the material but did not receive any guidance in checking their own understanding from peers.

What Checking for Understanding Is Not

Checking for understanding is not the final exam or the state achievement tests. While there is evidence that checking for understanding will improve the scores students receive on these types of assessments, they are not what we mean by "checking for understanding." Final exams and state standards tests are summative exams. They are designed to provide feedback on how the student performed after instruction.

FIGURE 1.1	Comparison of Formative and Summative Assessments	
Formative Assessments		**Summative Assessments**
To improve instruction and provide student feedback	**Purpose**	To measure student competency or mastery
Ongoing throughout unit	**When administered**	End of unit or course
To self-monitor understanding	**How students use results**	To gauge progress toward course- or grade-level goals and benchmarks
To check for understanding and provide additional instruction or intervention	**How teachers use results**	For grades, promotion

Checking for understanding is a systematic approach to formative assessment. Let's explore the difference between formative and summative assessment in greater detail. Figure 1.1 provides a comparison between the two assessment systems.

Formative assessments are ongoing assessments, reviews, and observations in a classroom. Teachers use formative assessment to improve instructional methods and provide student feedback throughout the teaching and learning process. For example, if a teacher observes that some students do not grasp a concept, he or she can design a review activity to reinforce the concept or use a different instructional strategy to reteach it. (At the very least, teachers should check for understanding every 15 minutes; we have colleagues who check for understanding every couple of minutes.) Likewise, students can monitor their progress by looking at their results on periodic quizzes and performance tasks. The results of formative assessments are used to modify and validate instruction.

Summative assessments are typically used to evaluate the effectiveness of instructional programs and services at the end of an academic year or at a predetermined time. The goal of summative assessments is to judge student competency after an instructional phase is complete. Summative evaluations are used to determine if students have mastered specific competencies and to identify instructional areas that need additional attention.

How Is Checking for Understanding Related to Other Teaching Initiatives?

There is no shortage of ideas for improving schools. An adaptation of a common saying hangs on our office wall that reads: "So many initiatives, so little time." This message reminds us on a daily basis that there is limited time to make progress; we have to pick and choose our initiatives wisely. Similarly, when our selected initiatives are conceptually linked, we know that we are more likely to implement them and see their widespread use. Let's consider how checking for understanding is related to some of the more common initiatives in education.

Understanding by Design

In 1998, Wiggins and McTighe proposed a curriculum model called Understanding by Design, in which curriculum and instruction are developed "backward." Teachers and curriculum developers learned to begin with the end in mind and plan accordingly. In other words, Wiggins and McTighe implored us to think about the outcomes, goals, and objectives we had for student learning first and then plan instruction and develop curriculum to close the gap between what students already know and what they need to know. A graphic representation of the stages in the backward curriculum design process can be found in Figure 1.2.

A significant part of the Understanding by Design model centers on the use of assessments that focus on student understanding. As Wiggins and McTighe note, "Because understanding develops as a result of ongoing inquiry and rethinking, the assessment of understanding should be thought of in terms of a collection of evidence over time instead of an event—a single moment-in-time test at the end of instruction" (1988, p. 13).

Differentiating Instruction

Carol Ann Tomlinson (1999) has challenged educators to differentiate instruction to meet the increasingly diverse needs of students. Teachers can differentiate the content, process, or products they use or expect from students. As noted in Tomlinson's model, assessment serves a critical role in teacher decision making. Teachers need to use a wide variety of assessment systems (and regularly check our

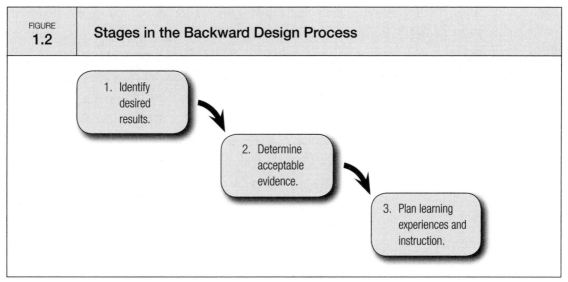

FIGURE 1.2	Stages in the Backward Design Process

Source: *Understanding by Design* (p. 18), by G. Wiggins and J. McTighe, 2005, ASCD. Used with permission.

students' understanding) to know whether or not our instructional interventions, modifications, accommodations, and extensions are working.

Checking for understanding presumes that students are able to demonstrate their understanding in different ways. This demands not only that products are differentiated but also that our ways of analyzing them are differentiated. Consider this example of a student's different responses to the same question.

Mariana, a 5th grader, was reluctant to speak in class. Mariana's teacher, Aida Allen, asked her to describe the character of Byron, the oldest brother in *The Watsons Go to Birmingham—1963* (Curtis, 1995). Byron is the kind of big brother who torments his younger siblings, sometimes making their lives miserable. However, his love for his brother and sister manifests itself in some surprising ways. Readers usually respond to Byron strongly, as his hurtful acts and flashes of kindness elevate him to the level of a realistic character. But in reply to Ms. Allen, Mariana merely mumbled, "Mean." Ms. Allen knew that Mariana had been enjoying the book and had overheard her talking to another member of her book club about it. A teacher who didn't understand checking for understanding might have cajoled Mariana for a minute or two and then moved on to another student who would supply a richer answer. But because she was interested in checking Mariana's understanding and not just filling the room with one student's answer, Ms. Allen later gave Mariana and a few other students character maps. "I'd like to know what you think about the main characters in this book and what evidence you have to support your opinions," she said. Mariana, uncomfortable with talking in class but engaged with the book, completed a character map of Byron in less than 10 minutes (see Figure 1.3). Her written response offered a far richer snapshot of her understanding than the monosyllabic answer she had supplied earlier. Because she was persistent in differentiating product to check for understanding, Ms. Allen could see that Mariana understood far more than she had originally demonstrated.

FIGURE 1.3	Mariana's Character Map

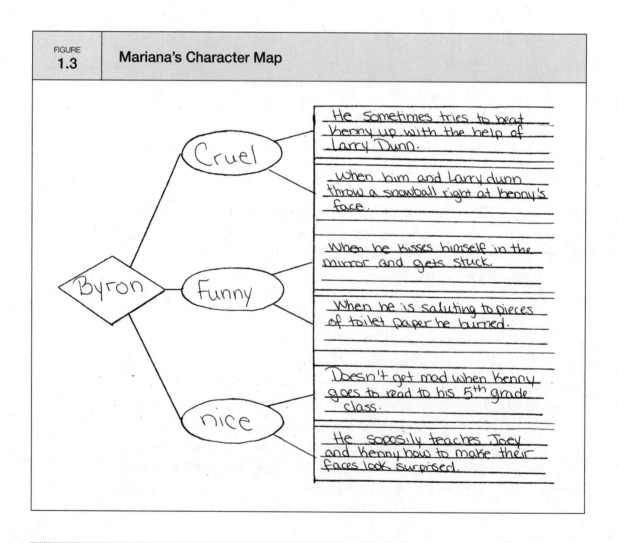

Framework for Intentional and Targeted Teaching™

Instruction and assessment are not simply random events in a classroom. They are linked in profound ways. It's the intentional and targeted instruction that provides students with experiences that teachers can use to check for understanding. And it's this same intentional and targeted instruction that allows teachers to address the errors and misconceptions that they unearth as they check for understanding. Intentional and targeted instruction is based on the gradual release of responsibility framework (Fisher & Frey, 2013b; Pearson & Gallagher, 1983). The framework we have developed includes four recursive phases: focused instruction, collaborative learning, guided instruction, and independent learning. In each phase, teachers can check for understanding. Additionally, each phase can be used to address student's errors or misconceptions, depending on the type of error and the number of students who made the error.

Focused instruction. As we noted earlier in this chapter, the purpose for learning must be established in a clear and coherent manner with students. A clearly articulated purpose provides teachers with guidance about checking for understanding and allows students to share responsibility for learning. When the purpose is not clear, or not agreed upon, students may complete a number of tasks yet not be motivated to assume responsibility. They may fail to understand the relevance of the content. Students practically beg for an established purpose when they ask, "Why do we gotta know this stuff?"

In addition to establishing purpose, focused instruction involves teacher modeling. Simply stated, students deserve an example of thinking and language required of the task before being asked to engage independently. In addition, there is evidence that humans are hard-wired to mimic or imitate other humans, which might explain why modeling is so effective. And further, there is evidence that scientists, historians, and mathematicians think differently and that this thinking is part of the discipline in which students need to be apprenticed (Shanahan & Shanahan, 2008).

Modeling requires that teachers provide an example of what happens in their minds as they solve problems, read, write, or complete tasks. Modeling is not an explanation or a time to question students, but rather an opportunity to demonstrate the ways in which experts think. Examples of modeling include:

• While reading a science text, Mr. Bonine stopped at the word "carnivore" and modeled his thinking about the Spanish word *carne,* which he said helped him remember that carnivores were the meat eaters.

• While thinking aloud about a text, Ms. Allen noted that the author introduced a problem. She said to her students, "Now here's a problem. I can predict that the solution to the problem will come next. That's how authors like to write, with a problem followed by a solution. I can take some notes using a problem and solution chart. Looking at the chart, I remember that in many cases, the solution to one problem creates new, often unexpected, problems. I wonder if that will be the case here."

• While looking at a table, Ms. Burow noted the column and row headings and how to find information accordingly and modeled the use of a legend to find information.

Each of these examples ensured that students got a glimpse inside their teachers' thinking and provided the teacher with fodder for checking for understanding. Mr. Bonine, for example, checked his students' ability to use context clues and word parts to solve unknown words, whereas Ms. Burow asked students to identify information from a chart using a legend.

Collaborative Learning. Regardless of the subject matter or content area, students learn more, and retain information longer, when they work collaboratively. Students who work in collaborative groups also appear more satisfied with their classes, complete more assignments, and generally like school better (Summers, 2006). Groups need time to interact, timelines, agreed-upon roles, and interdependent tasks to complete. In other words, collaborative learning tasks are not those that could have been accomplished by an individual. They need to be tasks that require interaction and the natural give-and-take of learning.

But the key to collaborative groups lies in accountability: each student must be accountable for some aspect of the collaborative learning task. Unfortunately, that's not always the case. We can all remember group work in which one student did all of the work and everyone else got credit. Not only does that prevent some students from learning, but the lack of accountability thwarts teachers' attempts to check for understanding and link instruction with formative assessment.

In her geometry class, Ms. Chen has students complete a collaborative poster for each proof they solve. Each student must contribute to the poster, and she knows if they contribute by the color of marker they use. Each student in the group of four has an assigned color, and students must sign their name to each poster. In addition to this collaborative task, the group must ensure that each of its members can explain the proof independently. This requires a significant amount of reteaching, negotiation, support, and trust. In other words, students are assuming responsibility for their learning and the learning of their peers.

Guided instruction. While purpose, modeling, and collaborative tasks are important aspects of learning, students also require guided instruction to be successful. We define guided instruction as the strategic use of questions, prompts, or cues designed to facilitate student thinking. Guided instruction should be based on assessment information. While guided instruction can be done with the whole class, our experience suggests that it is most effective with small groups. While students are engaged in collaborative tasks, the teacher can meet with a small group for guided instruction. Members of the group should be selected based on the data collected during checking for understanding. In her discussion with a group of students who misunderstood photosynthesis, Ms. Grant was able to use a series of questions and prompts to increase understanding.

Ms. Grant: Some of you thought that plants ate soil to grow. This is a very common misconception that we should talk about further. Do you remember the video we saw about photosynthesis? What role did soil play in that video?

Destini: Well, it wasn't about the dirt. It was about the sun and carbon dioxide.

Andrew: And how the plants make oxygen for humans.

Ms. Grant: Plants make oxygen for humans?

Andrew: Yeah. Well, I guess that they'd make oxygen even if there weren't humans.

Michael: It's called a by-product. They don't make oxygen for humans. They just make oxygen.

Ms. Grant: And what is left, once they've made this oxygen?

Destini: Carbon. They take in carbon dioxide and then give off oxygen, so carbon is left.

Ms. Grant: And what do you know about carbon?

Guided instruction provides teachers an opportunity to engage students in thinking, without telling them what to think. It's also an opportunity to scaffold their understanding before they're asked to complete tasks independently.

Independent learning. Independent learning, such as the application of information to a new situation, is the goal of schooling. Unfortunately, even a cursory look inside a typical classroom reveals that students are often asked to assume full responsibility for learning prematurely in the instructional cycle. Newly (or barely) learned tasks do not make for good independent learning. These require the clearly established purposes, teacher modeling, collaborative learning, and guided instruction found in sound classroom instruction. Instead, independent work should be reserved for review and reinforcement of previously taught concepts and applications. This phase of the instructional framework is ideal for the spiral review that so many educators know their students need but rarely get to implement. For example, an independent learning task to review the phases of the moon taught earlier in the school year should coincide with the new learning on the movement of planets around the sun. Thus, the independent learning task not only provides reinforcement of the phases, but also deepens their understanding of the patterns of movement in the sky and the ways they influence one another. In doing so, teachers can check for understanding of both current content and previously taught concepts.

Tips for Success

Checking for understanding completes the circle of assessment, planning, and instruction by providing teachers and students with evidence of learning. In addition, it is consistent with several other educational innovations, including Understanding by Design and differentiated instruction. Use these guiding questions to incorporate checking for understanding in your practice:

- Do I know what misconceptions or naïve assumptions my students possess?
- How do I know what they understand?
- What evidence will I accept for this understanding?
- How will I use their understandings to plan future instruction?

Teachers should plan intentional and targeted instruction, check for understanding, and then take action based on what the data says. Unfortunately, as

Schmoker (2006) notes, "an enormous proportion of daily lessons are simply never assessed—formally or informally. For the majority of lessons, no evidence exists by which a teacher could gauge or report on how well students are learning essential standards" (p. 16). Some tips to consider when integrating checking for understanding into your instructional plans include the following:

- Begin with the outcomes in mind. Know what you want your students to know and be able to do, and let them in on that secret.
- Create engaging lessons—focused instruction, collaborative learning, guided instruction, and independent learning—aligned with those outcomes.
- Plan to check for understanding, using a wide range of tools and strategies, on a regular basis.
- Take action based on the data that you collect. In other words, examine student responses to figure out what they know and what they still need to learn. And then plan additional instruction using some combination of focused instruction, collaborative learning, guided instruction, and independent learning to lead students to greater and greater success.

2

Using Oral Language to Check for Understanding

Humans have been using their voices to engage in critical and creative thinking for a long time—much longer, in fact, than they have used writing instruments. Sumerian cuneiforms, the first writing system, were not developed until about 4000 BCE (Ouaknin, 1999). This is a relatively short amount of time when you consider that humans have been communicating orally for at least 50,000 years (Ong, 1991). Interestingly, there are thousands of languages that have no written literature associated with them. As Ong (1991) notes:

> Indeed, language is so overwhelmingly oral that of all the many thousands of languages—possibly tens of thousands—spoken in the course of human history only around 106 have ever been committed to a degree sufficient to have produced literature, and most have never been written at all. Of the some 3,000 languages spoken that exist today only some 78 have a literature. (p. 7)

Humans have a long history of using oral language to communicate with one another. Oral language has served us well in conveying information that keeps members of our communities alive, healthy, safe, and fed. Most of all, verbal communication is our chief medium for understanding ourselves, others, and our world.

The classroom is no exception. In a book focused on the ways in which teachers and students interact, it seems appropriate to begin with the oldest language tradition. We'll define oral language first, explore its development, review some cautionary evidence of its misuse in the classroom, and then explore the ways in which oral language can be used in checking for understanding.

Oral Language Defined

We've adopted the speaking and listening definitions put forth by Cooper and Morreale:

> Speaking is the uniquely human act or process of sharing and exchanging information, ideas, and emotions using oral language. Whether in daily information interactions or in more formal settings, communicators are required to organize coherent messages, deliver them clearly, and adapt them to their listeners.
>
> Listening is the process of receiving, constructing meaning from, and responding to spoken and/or nonverbal messages. People call on different listening skills depending on whether their goal is to comprehend information, critique and evaluate a message, show empathy for the feelings expressed by others, or appreciate a performance. Taken together, the communication skills of speaking and listening, called *oral language,* form the basis for thinking. (2003, p. x)

Communication occurs across five distinct language registers (Figure 2.1). Speakers and listeners need to recognize these language registers, use them appropriately for the setting, and move fluidly between registers.

Effective speakers and listeners can move smoothly through the five registers, altering the variation to fit the context. The informal register, which is used with friends and family, results in the kind of shorthand communication that comes from shared experiences and background knowledge. Speakers often finish each other's sentences and leave much unspoken because a word or incomplete phrase triggers a shared understanding. But the consultative register is the one used most often in classroom discourse, and students' ability to engage in this register is an indicator of their academic success. The consultative register is the language of

FIGURE 2.1	**Language Registers**

Fixed or frozen. Fixed speech is reserved for traditions in which the language does not change. Examples of fixed speech include the Pledge of Allegiance, Shakespeare plays, and civil ceremonies such as weddings.

Formal. At the formal level, speech is expected to be presented in complete sentences with specific word usage. Formal language is the standard for work, school, and business and is more often seen in writing than in speaking. However, public speeches and presentations are expected to be delivered in a formal language register.

Consultative. The third level of language, consultative, is a formal register used in conversations. Less appropriate for writing, students often use consultative language in their interactions in the classroom.

Casual. This is the language that is used in conversation with friends. In casual speech, word choice is general and conversation is dependent upon nonverbal assists, significant background knowledge, and shared information.

Intimate. This is the language used by very close friends and lovers. Intimate speech is private and often requires a significant amount of shared history, knowledge, and experience.

school, as it requires detailed discussion and the use of academic language. The topics of classroom discussion are often far removed physically and temporally, such as volcanoes or the Revolutionary War. The speaker must provide a sufficient level of background knowledge in order to discuss these decontextualized phenomena. Speakers using this register fill in the background knowledge listeners will need, such as when the teacher is explaining a mathematics problem. Listeners integrate this background knowledge, ask questions, and provide explanations as well. Some students have difficulty in moving from the informal register of the playground to the consultative one needed in the classroom, and their performance suffers as a result.

Oral Language Development

Oral language development is not simply teaching children to speak. Oral language development focuses on students' ability to communicate more effectively. Oral language involves thinking, knowledge, and skills that develop across the life span. These are critical because "reading and writing float on a sea of talk" (Britton, 1970, p. 164).

A great deal is known about the oral language development of young children (see Paratore & Robertson, 2013). Researchers, parents, and teachers have articulated developmental milestones for children's acquisition of oral communication skills. Many of us are familiar with these early milestones as babies learn to smile, approximate sounds, and then use words. Toddlers integrate new words each day and engage in imaginative play, tell stories, and laugh at simple jokes. Upon entry into school, young children must develop their consultative register. Early childhood programs are so important to school success in part because they provide their students with opportunities to immerse themselves in this register (Strickland & Riley-Ayers, 2006).

There is a significant body of evidence on the importance of attending to oral language development for English language learners across the K–12 spectrum (Greenfader & Brouillette 2013). Given that oral language is the foundation of print literacy, it seems reasonable to suggest that all teachers, and especially those who teach English language learners, focus on speaking and listening in the classroom.

Misuses of Oral Language in the Classroom

Regardless of the size of the school, its demographics, the age of the teaching staff, or any other factor that we can think of, oral language will be used in the classroom. People will talk and listen—that's a given. The ways in which this talking and listening are used are the real key. There are at least three areas that we should address before continuing our discussion of the use of oral language in checking for understanding: poverty, language, and perceived skill level; gender differences; and the Initiate-Respond-Evaluate model of questioning.

Poverty, Language, and Perceived Skill Level

In classrooms where there are increased numbers of students living in poverty, teachers talk more and students talk less (Lingard, Hayes, & Mills, 2003). In addition, there is an increased focus on basic skills in these classrooms and less attention to critical and creative thinking (Stipek, 2004). Teachers of struggling students usually offer them "less exciting instruction, less emphasis on meaning and conceptualization, and more rote drill and practice activities" than do teachers of high-performing or heterogeneous groups and classes (Cotton, 1989).

English language learners in many classrooms are asked easier questions or no questions at all (Guan Eng Ho, 2005). Several decades ago, Flanders (1970) noted that teachers of high-achieving students talked 55 percent of the class time. He compared them with teachers of low-achieving students who monopolized class time, talking at least 80 percent of the time.

In other words, the amount of teacher versus student talk in a classroom varies by the demographics of the students. In addition, students who live in poverty, are English language learners, have disabilities, or are otherwise at risk in school spend more of their time on basic skills and less time engaged in activities, lessons, or inquiry that requires language and fosters creative and critical thinking.

Gender Differences

Interestingly, gender also plays a role in how much talk there is in a classroom. While there are debates on which gender is at greater risk for school failure and lack of engagement (Sadker & Zittleman, 2009), there is clear evidence that the amount of time that girls spend participating orally in class decreases as they get older (Orenstein, 1994). In addition, there is evidence that teachers call on boys more often than girls, ask boys more higher-order questions, give boys more extensive feedback, and use longer wait time with boys than with girls (Sadker & Sadker, 1995).

The Initiate-Respond-Evaluate Model

In classrooms across the country, teachers ask students questions and students respond. The Initiate-Respond-Evaluate model of questioning dominates classroom discourse (Cazden, 1988). In this model, the teacher asks a question, specific students are called on to answer the question, and the teacher evaluates the response. A typical interaction might look something like this:

> *Teacher:* Why did the Puritans leave England? (*Initiate*)
> *Student:* Because they were not treated right because of their religion. (*Respond*)
> *Teacher:* Yes. (*Evaluate*) And why else? (*Initiate*)

While this interaction requires oral language, it focuses on "guess what's in the teacher's head" or what the teacher already knows, not on critical thinking by the whole group. In addition, when one student is provided the opportunity to answer, the ability to check for understanding with the larger group is lost. Cazden (1988) suggests that teachers ask themselves two questions about the discourse in their classrooms:

- How do patterns of talk in the classroom affect the quality of students' educational opportunities and outcomes?
- How is discourse used as a support for deeper student learning?

Let's explore these questions as we consider the ways in which teachers can proactively and positively use oral language to check for understanding.

Oral Language Strategies in Checking for Understanding

Accountable Talk

How often have you assigned a partner discussion topic to students, only to hear the conversation devolve into a chat about weekend activities, a new movie, or the lunch menu? Often these students are not being willfully disobedient, but rather lack the skills necessary to conduct a meaningful conversation about an academic topic. Accountable talk is a framework for teaching students about discourse in order to enrich these interactions. First developed by Lauren Resnick (2000) and a team of researchers at the Institute for Learning at the University of Pittsburgh, accountable talk describes the agreements students and their teacher commit to as they engage in partner conversations. These include the following guidelines:

- Stay on topic.
- Use information that is accurate and appropriate for the topic.
- Think deeply about what the partner has to say.

We consider accountable talk to be crucial to classroom discourse because it creates shared expectations for all academic communication in the classroom. The three principles are equally relevant in a book club meeting, a Socratic seminar, or a whole-class discussion.

Students are taught how to be accountable to one another and to their learning using techniques that forward the conversation and deepen their understanding of the topic at hand. The Institute for Learning website (www.instituteforlearning.org) describes five indicators of accountable talk; we have added an example after each:

- Press for clarification and explanation: "Could you describe what you mean?"
- Require justification of proposals and challenges: "Where did you find that information?"
- Recognize and challenge misconceptions: "I don't agree because. . . ."
- Demand evidence for claims and arguments: "Can you give me an example?"
- Interpret and use each other's statements: "David suggested. . . ."

These communication skills are invaluable for students using inquiry as a way to engage in active learning. Teachers fostering accountable talk in the classroom can monitor the use of these indicators by listening to partners exchange information. In addition, the questions students ask of one another should inform the next segment of teacher-led instruction.

Sixth grade teacher Ricardo Montoya monitors partner conversations to make teaching decisions. During one lesson, he introduced the concept of physical and chemical weathering to students, assigned students to groups, and asked the partners to identify examples of the two types of weathering using a series of photographs. As Mr. Montoya listened in on the students' conversations, he noticed that several partners were asking clarifying questions of one another concerning a photograph of acid rain. A few partners felt it was an example of physical weathering because of the force of the water. Many others described it as chemical weathering due to the acidic quality of the rain. Mr. Montoya asked partners to share their conversations, including their disagreements, with the rest of the class. He then led a class discussion on the possibility of considering acid rain as an example of both chemical and physical weathering. Mr. Montoya's attention to the students' conversations helped him to make the next instructional step in his lesson.

Mr. Montoya understands that students will not engage in accountable talk simply because they are asked to do so. "It took me awhile to realize that I have to model the principles [of accountable talk] in my discussions with the class." The conversational moves he employs regularly as a teacher become the way in which students talk with one another (Michaels, O'Connor, Hall, & Resnick, 2010). "It's kind of funny to hear them sounding more like me as the year goes on," he chuckled. "When I hear them ask one another to 'say more about that' or make connections between the comments of other speakers, I know they are channeling the way I facilitate discussion with them."

Language Frames

Often students need support to engage in the types of conversations we want them to have. Of course, modeling conversational moves is important, as is teaching the components of accountable talk. In addition, the use of sentence or language frames can provide students with another level of scaffolding. When teachers provide these types of scaffolds, the language demands of the task are reduced and both students and teachers can focus on the content. This is important in checking for understanding as teachers need to know if students understand the content and need more practice with language or if they have errors or misconceptions that need to be addressed.

College composition experts Gerald Graff and Cathy Birkenstein (2006) recommend the use of sentence frames (they call them templates) as an effective way for developing students' academic writing skills. They defend the use of frames or templates by noting:

> After all, even the most creative forms of expression depend on established patterns and structures. Most songwriters, for instance, rely on a time-honored verse-chorus-verse pattern, and few people would call Shakespeare uncreative because he didn't invent the sonnet or dramatic forms that he used to such dazzling effect. . . . Ultimately, then, creativity and originality lie not in the avoidance of established forms, but in the imaginative use of them. (pp. 10–11)

As Graff and Birkenstein note, frames and templates help students incorporate established norms of academic writing. We use these frames to teach students how to talk with one another. Often, we organize the frames based on the expected cognitive move. For example, the sentence frames in Figure 2.2 are organized around the components of argumentation.

As part of their discussion of nuclear chemistry, the students in Marla Brandywine's class used the argumentation sentence frames to make their claims and provide evidence. For example, Yusuf said, "The reason I believe that we should

FIGURE 2.2	Language Frames for Argumentation
Making a claim	I observed _____ when _____. I compared _____ and _____. I noticed _____, when _____. The effect of _____ on _____ is _____.
Providing evidence	The evidence I use to support _____ is _____. I believe _____ (statement) because _____ (justification). I know that _____ is _____ because _____. Based on _____, I think _____. Based upon _____, my hypothesis is _____.
Asking for evidence	I have a question about _____. Does _____ have more _____? What causes _____ to _____? Can you show me where you found the information about _____?
Offering a counterclaim	I disagree _____ because _____. The reason I believe _____ is _____. The facts that support my idea are _____. In my opinion _____. One difference between my idea and yours is _____.
Inviting speculation	I wonder what would happen if _____. I have a question about _____. Let's find out how we can test these samples for _____. We want to test _____ to find out if _____. If I change _____, (variable in experiment) then I think _____ will happen, because _____. I wonder why _____? What caused _____? How would this be different if _____? What do you think will happen if _____ / next?
Reaching consensus	I agree _____ because _____. How would this be different if _____? We all have the same idea about _____.

Source: Ross, D., Fisher, D., & Frey, N. (2009). The art of argumentation. *Science and Children, 47*(3), 28–31.

still work on nuclear chemistry is because it is used in medicine, like in imaging." Olivia agreed, saying, "I agree that scientists should still work on this because it also is used to help people with cancer."

Noticing Nonverbal Cues

Another way that teachers use oral language to check for understanding involves noticing the nonverbal cues that students give. While it may seem a stretch to include nonverbal cues in typical oral language interactions, remember that a significant portion of our communication comes from facial expression, eye movement, and such (see White & Gardner, 2011). Students in our classrooms often let us know that they do or do not understand something through nonverbal cues, which may be as simple as the look on one's face or as complex as throwing one's hands in the air (in triumph over a math problem or in agony over a reading assignment). As a teacher, you can use nonverbal cues to determine if your students look puzzled, harried, or bored. With practice, you will find yourself noticing and responding to these nonverbal cues while teaching.

Fifth grade teacher Amanda Chavez uses a daily shared reading lesson to model her thinking and comprehension strategies for students. She knows that her focused instruction and modeling will provide students with increasingly complex ways of thinking about texts. During her shared reading about Sojourner Truth from *Americans Who Tell the Truth* (Shetterly, 2005), Ms. Chavez noticed that Angel had a puzzled look on her face. Ms. Chavez paused in her reading and added some information that she had obtained from another text, watching Angel's face the whole time for signs of understanding. When Ms. Chavez said, "It seems strange now, but during the times of slavery, people could sell children who were born into slavery," Angel's face changed noticeably. It became clear that Angel couldn't grasp the text about Sojourner Truth's life until she had the understanding that people have sold children.

Value Lineups

Many students master the skill of explaining their own position on a topic, but fewer learn the art of listening to positions that differ from their own. However, this ability is at the heart of meaningful discourse in the classroom and is essential to all learning. In a truly learner-centered classroom, there is a free exchange of ideas that results in arriving at solutions to problems. Active learning results not from a knowledge dump emanating from the teacher alone but from a deeper understanding of the nuances and shades of gray that elevate knowledge.

Value lineups help students to develop in-depth knowledge by enabling them to explore core concepts and understand problems by having them first analyze their beliefs and then listen to the positions held by others. The value lineup is a structure for fostering peer discourse based on students' opinions about an academic topic (Kagan, 1994). Students are asked to evaluate a statement and instructed to line up according to their degree of agreement or disagreement with the statement. After forming a single line, the queue is then folded in half so that the students who most strongly agreed and disagreed with one another are now face to face. Students then discuss their reasons for their positions and listen to the perspectives of their partners. This cultivates a broader understanding of the distinctions of understanding on a topic.

When Deborah Choi's 10th grade biology students were beginning a unit on the use of cloning, she asked them to consider their values and beliefs about cloning in reaction to this statement: "Scientists should be allowed to pursue research in cloning." Ms. Choi's students then placed themselves on the wall of the classroom where the numbers 1 through 5 were displayed in a Likert-type scale. She reminded them that a 5 meant they strongly agreed, 4 meant they agreed, 3 meant they were not sure, 2 meant they disagreed, and 1 indicated that they strongly disagreed.

The students spent the next two minutes lining up according to their opinions. Ms. Choi then located the 18th student in line (the halfway point in this class of 36) and folded the line in half. Now the first student spoke to the 36th student, the second spoke to the 35th, and so on. Ms. Choi walked the line, listening to their conversations about why they agreed or disagreed with scientific research on cloning. She heard Anne, who strongly agreed, explaining to Paul, who strongly disagreed, about her recent trip with her family to Yosemite: "There's this project to clone the champion trees of the country so that they can be planted in other places, especially in cities." She went on to explain that champion trees are the largest of their species and possess unique genetic features that make them more durable. Paul remarked that he never thought of cloning trees, only of humans, even though Ms. Choi's question did not mention this.

After several minutes of conversation, Ms. Choi instructed students to return to their seats. The lively debate continued, but important information from multiple perspectives was shared in the discussion. A number of factors were introduced to the problem of cloning, including benefits and moral and religious objections. By using the value lineup, Ms. Choi was able to assess preconceived notions, background knowledge, and gaps in information. In addition, her students were challenged to consider other perspectives on the topic.

A variation on the value lineup is called Opinion Stations. Rather than have students line up along a continuum, students meet with others who share their opinion. Typically, teachers post four statements in the corners of the classroom: Strongly Agree, Agree, Disagree, and Strongly Disagree. Opinion stations do not typically provide for a neutral response but rather require that students take a position.

For example, during the discussion of the book *Wonder* (Palacio, 2012), the students in Amy Tanaka's class were asked if they believed that the character's parent's decision to send him to school was a good one. They had just read the first part of the text, having met the main character, Auggie, who was born with a facial deformity that prevented him from attending mainstream school. In Auggie's words, "I won't describe what I look like. Whatever you're thinking, it's probably worse" (p. 3). The students moved to the corner that represented their thinking. In the strongly agree corner, students discussed Auggie's right to attend school. In the strongly disagree corner, students noted that Auggie would probably be teased and bullied. Ms. Tanaka, listening in on her students' conversations, knew that they were understanding the complexity of the situation and were able to clarify their thinking with their peers.

Retellings

Retellings are new accounts or adaptations of a text that allow students to consider information and then summarize, orally, what they understand about this information. Retellings require that students processing large segments of text think about the sequence of ideas or events and their importance. Inviting students to retell what they have just heard or read is a powerful way of checking for understanding (Hoyt, 2008). Cambourne (1998) argues that retelling is a more effective postreading activity than teacher questioning.

To be effective, students need to be taught the procedures of retelling. Understanding these processes helps establish purpose in reading and guides students' attention to key information from the text that they can use in their retellings. Figure 2.3 provides a number of variations on retellings, some of which will be discussed in the next chapter on using writing to check for understanding. In introducing the retelling technique, teachers should

1. Explain that the purpose of a retelling is to re-create the text in your own words.
2. Ask students to discuss the ways in which they talk about their favorite movie. Make the connection between talking about the movie and talking about a piece of text.
3. Model a retelling from a short piece of familiar text for students. If students know the piece of text well, they can compare the original with the retelling.
4. After the modeled retelling, ask students to discuss the similarities and differences between the original and the retelling.
5. Select a new piece of text, read it aloud, and create a retelling as a group. Again, ask students to discuss the similarities and differences between the original and the retelling.

As students become increasingly familiar with retellings, they can be used to check for understanding.

FIGURE 2.3	Variations on Retellings
Oral to Oral Oral to Written Oral to Video	Listens to a selection and retells it orally Listens to a selection and retells it in writing (summary) Listens to a selection and creates a video of it
Reading to Oral Reading to Written Reading to Video	Reads a selection and retells it orally Reads a selection and retells it in writing (summary) Reads a selection and creates a video of it
Viewing to Oral Viewing to Written Viewing to Video	Views a film and retells it orally Views a film and retells it in writing (summary) Views a film and creates a video of it

Fourth grade teacher Aida Allen used the story retelling rubric found in Figure 2.4 to check her students' understanding of fiction and story grammar. She introduced the rubric after reading aloud *The Day the Crayons Quit* (Daywalkt, 2013). As a class, they created a retelling. Ms. Allen then facilitated the students in a discussion of the rubric, and they evaluated their group retelling using this tool. Next, Ms. Allen gave each group of four students different picture books. Their task was to read the book together and create a small-group retelling.

FIGURE 2.4	**Retelling Rubric for Fiction**			
Element	**Exceeds Standards (2)**	**Meets Standards (1)**	**Needs Improvement (0)**	**Score**
Characters	Your retelling describes the characters so that others have a good idea of what they are like.	Your retelling names the characters but does not describe much about them.	Your retelling confuses the identity of the characters or does not name them. Think about who was in the story and how they acted.	
Setting	Your retelling helps others get a clear idea of when and where the story took place.	Your retelling provides some details about where and when the story took place.	Your retelling needs to describe when and where the story took place.	
Problem	Your retelling describes the problem, why this problem occurred, and how it might be solved.	Your retelling names the problem but not how it occurred or might be solved.	Your retelling needs to describe the problem, how the problem developed, and how it might be solved.	
Solution	Your retelling focuses on how the characters solved the problem.	Your retelling includes some of the important events that led to the solution and most are in the correct order.	Your retelling needs to focus on the major events and how these events led to the solution to the problem.	
Delivery	Your retelling uses good rhythm, fluency, expression, and gestures. Your voice changes for different characters.	Your rhythm and expression are good most of the time and you use some gestures. Your voice changes for some of the characters.	Your retelling needs to include expression and gestures. Your voice should change for different characters.	

As each group presented their retelling, another group (assigned by Ms. Allen) used the retelling rubric to provide feedback. Ms. Allen reminded her students after each retelling that "we are all learning how to use the story retelling rubric—let's all help each other get really good at this."

Following several practices with using the story retelling rubric in groups, students were asked to meet with Ms. Allen individually to discuss and retell information from the books they were reading in their literature circles. The focus was on dog stories and included *Shiloh* (Naylor, 1991), *Where the Red Fern Grows: The Story of Two Dogs and a Boy* (Rawls, 1961), and *My Dog Skip* (Morris, 1995). Ms. Allen used the information she gathered during student retellings of the books they were reading to plan individual interventions as well as some additional small-group guided instruction and whole-class focused instruction.

Ms. Allen noted that her students rarely used dialogue during their retellings to discuss characters and the problems they faced. In subsequent shared readings, she modeled several retellings using character dialogue to address this whole-class need. Similarly, she noted that one student, Miriam, had difficulty with sequence; she met with Miriam during reading conferences and helped her use a graphic organizer to record events in order.

U.S. history teacher Jamie Ryan used the informational text retelling rubric shown in Figure 2.5 in her class. During the unit on the 1906 San Francisco earthquake, students read a number of primary source documents, including the proclamation by the mayor dated April 18, 1906. They recorded their retellings digitally and loaded them onto the course website. One student correctly noted in his retelling that the mayor had authorized the police to kill any looters they found. He also pointed out that the mayor's proclamation gave the police "exceptional powers—they could legally kill any person for ANY crime." The rubric allowed Ms. Ryan an opportunity to check her students' understanding of the various texts they read and to determine areas of need for each student.

Think-Pair-Share and Think-Pair-Square

Think-Pair-Share is a cooperative discussion strategy that allows students to discuss their responses with a peer before sharing with the whole class. Developed by Lyman (1981) and colleagues, there are three stages of student action:

FIGURE 2.5	Retelling Rubric for Informational Text			
Element	**Exceeds Standards (2)**	**Meets Standards (1)**	**Needs Improvement (0)**	**Score**
Key Ideas	Your retelling identifies all of the key ideas from the text.	Your retelling identifies a number of key ideas from the text.	Your retelling needs to identify and describe the key ideas from the text.	
Details	Your retelling helps others understand the text by providing details for each key idea.	Your retelling provides some details for some of the key ideas.	Your retelling needs to link details with key ideas.	
Sequence	Your retelling identifies a clear sequence of information that helps the listener understand the information.	Your retelling provides information in a sequence, but the sequence is slightly confused or out of order.	Your retelling needs to have a sequence that helps the listener understand the information.	
Conclusion	Your retelling ends with a conclusion that is directly linked to the information you provided.	Your retelling includes a concluding statement.	Your retelling needs to focus on the major idea from the text and needs to summarize the information gathered.	
Delivery	You use good rhythm, fluency, expression, and gestures.	Your rhythm and expression are good most of the time and you use some gestures.	Your retelling needs to include expression and gestures.	

1. **Think.** The teacher engages students' thinking with a question, prompt, reading, visual, or observation. The students should take a few minutes (not seconds) just to *think* about the question.

2. **Pair.** Using designated partners, students *pair* up to discuss their respective responses. They compare their thoughts and identify the responses they think are the best, most intriguing, most convincing, or most unique.

3. **Share.** After students talk in pairs for a few moments, the teacher asks pairs to *share* their thinking with the rest of the class.

Naturally, there are opportunities to check for understanding throughout the Think-Pair-Share activity. The teacher can listen in as pairs discuss their responses and can note the ways in which pairs share their responses.

In her 2nd grade class, Yazmine Sanchez invited her students to think about a person who made a difference. This introduction to a major 2nd grade social studies theme served to activate her students' background knowledge and to help them make connections with the curriculum they were about to study. After a few moments of thinking time, Ms. Sanchez asked her students to turn to a partner and talk about the person they were thinking of. Ms. Sanchez listened in on several students' pair conversations, noting their personal connections to the topic. She then invited pairs to share with the whole class. But she wasn't done yet; she continued this process with several additional questions, including the following:

- What did this person do that makes you think he or she made a difference?
- Who else do you know who made a difference?
- What characteristics are shared by people who make a difference?

With each question, Ms. Sanchez asked her students to think first, engage in a partner conversation, and then share their ideas with the whole class. As they did so, Ms. Sanchez made notes about what her students already knew, what misconceptions they had, and how they used language to express their ideas. Her checking for understanding was used to collect information that she could use in her instruction throughout the unit.

Similarly, high school government teacher Angie Jenkins uses Think-Pair-Share to engage her students in current government issues each day. During a discussion about immigration policy in the United States, students noted the potential changes to the policy. The variation Ms. Jenkins uses with her high school seniors is that they have to share their partner's thinking, not their own ideas. She does this to ensure that her students are listening and thinking as their partner talks, rather than forming rebuttal arguments. In one of the discussions on the changes to the immigration policy, Malik said, "My partner is going to participate in the walk-out because she thinks that it's important to send a message and cost the government money. By not being here at school that day, she'll cost people money." Another student indicated, "Arian is going to come to school because she says that her mom came here to make sure she got an education."

The Think-Pair-Share time provides Ms. Jenkins with an opportunity to determine whether her students understand the current events that affect their lives and to ascertain if students still have any misunderstandings about these events in terms of government policy. She is interested not in changing their views of current events, but in making sure that they can think critically about the events that will shape their experiences as adults.

There are several variations on this general approach to encouraging student-to-student interaction. For example, Think-Pair-Square follows the first two steps of the Think-Pair-Share, but then requires student partners to join another group to continue their conversation with a larger number of participants. This increases the opportunity each student has to talk compared with whole-class sharing. For example, during their investigation of heart-related diseases and conditions, the students in Mark Mellman's health class discussed the similarities and differences between heart attacks and strokes. The students were provided time think about the two and then shared their thinking with their partner. After several minutes, Mr. Mellman asked each partnership to join another and to share their thinking with the other team. As he walked around the room, he heard groups of students talking about the impact of diet and smoking. He also noted that most students understood the different locations of the two events and the role of blood supply. Of concern, he heard several groups talking about the pain involved in both heart attacks and strokes, and knew that he had to address this misconception with his students.

Novel Ideas Only

Novel Ideas Only is a useful instructional tool teachers can use to check for understanding in a group setting. While this tool may not provide individual, student-level information about understanding, it is useful in helping teachers determine if they need to reteach content to the group. As such, this strategy is often used as a closure activity at the end of a period of instruction.

The procedure is fairly simple. First, the teacher poses a question or a task; typically, students are asked to make a list of at least three items. Students then individually respond on a scrap piece of paper. When they have done so, students stand up. The teacher then randomly calls on a student to share one of his or her ideas from the paper. Students check off any items that are said by another student and sit down when all of their ideas have been shared with the group, whether or not they were the one to share them. The teacher continues to call on students until they are all seated. As the teacher listens to the ideas or information shared by students, he or she can determine if there is a general level of understanding or if there are gaps in students' thinking.

Third grade teacher Mandi Smith uses this technique as her daily closure activity. During her unit of study on insects, she asked her students to make a list of the characteristics that distinguish insects from other creatures on Earth. She said that she has to be very specific or her 3rd graders will write comparisons with dinosaurs, space people, and other things not found on Earth. Ms. Smith was pleased to learn that the vast majority of her students understood that insects have three body parts, the head, abdomen, and thorax; that they have eyes and one pair of antennae and mouthparts; that they have six legs; that their skeleton is an exoskeleton; and that they have an open circulatory system. Ms. Smith noted, however, that the students did not discuss wings, what the antennae do, or how the mouthparts and legs have adapted. She knew that she would need to review this information the following day to ensure that her students grasped it.

Similarly, health educator Stacey Everson uses Novel Ideas Only at the end of her classroom discussions. During a 9th grade health education lesson, Ms. Everson asked students to identify the risk factors for suicide. After writing individually for several minutes, the students stood up, and Ms. Everson invited them to share one at a time. She analyzed their responses and noted the factors that most students had on their own pages. She also noted areas that were not addressed by students and provided the class with supplemental readings on the topic as well as a yellow ribbon card (see www.yellowribbon.org for details), which provides students with permission to ask for help as well as tells them what to do if someone else uses the help card.

Tips for Success

There are a number of ways that teachers can use oral language—speaking and listening—to check for understanding. Through careful planning and analysis of student responses, teachers can close the gap between what students need to know and what they already know.

Some tips to consider as you use oral language to check for understanding include the following:

• Students need to do a lot of talking in the classroom. Having clear expectations and procedures for student-to-student interaction is important, and providing time for students to work collaboratively is critical.

• Provide students with language frames to scaffold their use of academic language. This allows teachers to focus students' content knowledge and provides students an opportunity to apprentice with academic language.

• Listen in on student discussions. Notice errors and misconceptions that can be addressed through additional instruction.

• Interweave oral language opportunities with instruction throughout a unit, not just near the beginning or end of the lesson.

3

Using Questions to Check for Understanding

The art of questioning is central to the practice of teaching. Well-crafted questions are a great way for teachers to determine what students know, need to know, and misunderstand. Poorly crafted questions are a waste of time, for both students and teachers, because they do not provide students with an opportunity to think, nor do they provide teachers with information that they can use to plan instruction and intervention. There is a wide range of question types that teachers can use to assess students' understanding. These will be discussed later in this chapter. There are also a number of ways for teachers to respond to students when they have answered incorrectly. These will also be addressed in this chapter. Before discussing these aspects of questioning, we focus our attention on effective questioning techniques.

Checking for understanding through questioning should not be thought of as a simple two-step process (question and answer), but rather as a complex progression as the teacher formulates and then listens to the response of the learner. Walsh and Sattes (2011) describe five distinct steps of the questioning process: Preparing the question, presenting the question, prompting student responses, processing student responses, and reflecting on questioning practices.

The first step is to formulate the question. In particular, the teacher must determine the purpose of the question itself. Is it an elicitation question to orient students? For example, the 4th grade geography teacher who points to Pennsylvania on a map of the United States and asks, "What's the name of this state?" is asking an elicitation question. This allows the teacher to follow up with questions about geographical features of the area, such as its rivers and mountains. A question can also serve the purpose of recalling information, such as when the same geography teacher asks, "What are the two largest cities in Pennsylvania?" In this case, students must recall what they know about the state, about urban centers, and about cities in Pennsylvania. Both questions are examples of factual knowledge but neither is likely to promote enduring understanding. It is necessary, however, for students to possess this information. A third type of question asks students to apply information in a novel way. For example, the geography teacher might ask, "What are the advantages and disadvantages of locating the state capital in Harrisburg?" In any case, the teacher needs to be clear on the type of knowledge the question assesses and not fall into the trap of confusing recognition or recall for application. Additional information about types of questions is presented later in this chapter.

After formulating the question, the teacher must determine the format of the desired response and who will provide it. Will it be a choral answer, where all students respond together? Is it a partner discussion question? If so, the teacher should preface the question itself with information about the response format so that students know what they will do with the question before it is asked. If it is to be answered by an individual student, teachers should announce the student's name before asking the question. This alerts the learner to the expected response and avoids using the question as a means for classroom management.

Once the question has been asked, students need time to process the answer. Commonly referred to as "wait time," pausing for three to five seconds allows learners time to digest the question, retrieve information, and formulate a response (Rowe, 1986). This is particularly useful for English language learners who may still be code switching (i.e., mentally translating the question from English to their primary language, then translating their answer to English).

If a student is unable to respond or responds incorrectly, the teacher can provide scaffolds so that the student can arrive at the correct answer. It is possible that the student does not understand the question itself or that he or she is unable to retrieve the information needed to reply. For example, the teacher might cue the student, "Look at the graph on page 252 of your textbook." Alternatively, the teacher might prompt the student, "How does the largest bar on the graph on page 252 of your textbook help you to find your answer?" Additional information about prompts and cues will be presented later in this chapter.

Once the student has answered, the teacher must use the response to make decisions about what will occur next. Feedback, which includes praise, should be offered to the student; it may include affirmation of a correct response or elaboration on an incomplete answer. It is useful to think about scaffolds as follow-up probes when responding to incomplete or incorrect answers. These follow-up probes serve as a means for teaching students how to use information to formulate answers. Ultimately, the art and science of teaching require the ability to use scaffolds effectively to cultivate student learning. The challenge is to use the right scaffold to assist the learner in doing the cognitive work (Wood, Bruner, & Ross, 1976).

The final step to effective questioning involves analyzing the techniques used as well as the content of the students' answers. One tool to determine equitable distribution of questions is charting who answers and how often. We have done this using a seating chart inside a clear binder sleeve. As students answer, we place a check on the chart using a marker. This is also useful for identifying students who are not participating and for identifying patterns such as favoring one section of the room over another or calling on boys more frequently than girls. The content of the questions is important, too, and an audio recording of a lesson can assist in determining whether the range of questions a teacher asks reflects the types of knowledge taught.

Perhaps the most important practice is analyzing students' responses. Again, a recording can be useful for engaging in this reflective practice. It is easy to be lured into thinking of students' answers as dichotomous—either correct or incorrect. However, it is essential to keep in mind that a student's answer reflects everything he or she knows and does not know at that particular moment. In other words, an incorrect answer is completely logical to the learner, even if it seems irrational to the teacher. The challenge is to analyze the incorrect answer to hypothesize what the student understands and does not understand, because then the teacher can determine what needs to occur next.

As you listen to a recording of one of your lessons, note the answers your students supplied and how you handled incorrect responses. How often did you scaffold their answers? Were there times when you rephrased a question to clarify understanding? Were there times when a clue would have been more useful? Sometimes a student is not able to answer even when supports have been offered. In this case, it may be wise to ask another student the question and then return to the first student to ensure understanding.

Misuses of Questioning in the Classroom

As noted in the previous chapter, one difficulty is that the questioning rarely advances beyond the Initiate-Respond-Evaluate cycle (Cazden, 1988; see Chapter 2). In the hands of less able teachers, questioning can devolve into interrogation, as students struggle to guess what's in the teacher's head. This does not allow the teacher to gain a full understanding of students' thinking and may result in instruction in basic facts that students are expected to recall. That's not to say that understanding basic facts is bad. Students should develop their understanding of factual information. It's just that this type of questioning prevents the teacher from delving into student thinking such that errors and misconceptions can be addressed.

In addition, there is evidence that a vocal minority of students dominate classroom conversations and questioning, while less assertive students rarely participate (Brophy & Evertson, 1974). This difference not only results in behavioral difficulties and marginalized students, but also affects the ability of the teacher to check for understanding. After all, knowing that six or seven students understand is not the same as knowing that 32 do. Therefore, it is essential to use effective questioning techniques to elicit richer evidence of understanding. These questioning techniques should be coupled with instructional approaches that maximize participation in classroom discourse.

A third misuse of questions in the classroom relates to who asks the questions. Of course, teachers need to ask a wide range of questions to check for understanding. But in effective classrooms, students also learn to ask questions of themselves and their peers. And these questions should be more than recall and Initiate-Respond-Evaluate. Students will ask questions of themselves and others that are consistent with the questions they are asked by teachers. If they are consistently required to respond to questions that privilege evidence in the response, they will become used to that and expect it of themselves and others. However, if they are regularly asked yes/no questions, they will ask these types of questions as well.

Developing Authentic Questions

As we have noted, teachers are going to ask questions of students. Questions are a great way of checking for understanding. The important thing is to ensure that the questions engage students in deeper thinking and don't merely prompt them to recall information that they have read or been told.

One way to make certain that the questions we ask engage students' creative and critical thinking is to plan them in advance using an organizational structure such as Bloom's (1956) taxonomy. Figure 3.1 provides a review of Bloom's taxonomy and descriptive words and prompts related to each level. It is important to keep in mind that a taxonomy is not necessarily a hierarchy, and that Bloom never discussed so-called lower-order and higher-order questions. Rather, a taxonomy is a way of classifying information, in this case, types of knowledge. Therefore, knowledge and comprehension questions are directed at gathering a specific type of input. This information is necessary to apply, analyze, synthesize, and evaluate. The criticism of knowledge and comprehension questions concerns the extent to which they are used at the expense of others. As we discussed earlier, recognition and recall are requisite skills, but they do not encompass the limits of understanding. Bloom's taxonomy is an excellent tool for developing questions that represent the range of knowledge that should be taught in the classroom.

Sixth grade teacher Alexandria Ollendorff uses Bloom's taxonomy with her students to encourage them to ask and answer their own questions. She introduces prompts like the ones listed in Figure 3.1 to guide her students. They play a daily game in which groups of students create questions based on the information they are studying that day. The questions they create are used for a Jeopardy-type game, with the number of points determined by the level of the question according to the taxonomy (knowledge is 1 point; evaluation is 6 points). During a unit about ancient Egypt and their gods, some of the questions one group created included the following:

- Who was Ra? (remember)
- Why do some gods and goddesses have animal heads? (understand)
- How do you feel about mummification? (evaluate)
- Compare and contrast Isis, Ptah, and Horus in terms of their importance to the Egyptian people. (analyze)
- What role should gods play in setting rules for people? (evaluate)

FIGURE 3.1	Bloom's Taxonomy for the 21st Century	
Level	**Key Words**	**Prompts**
Remember: Recall data or information.	define, describe, identify, know, label, list, match, name, outline, recall, recognize, reproduce, select, state	Where is . . . What did . . . Who was . . . When did . . . How many . . . Locate it in the story . . . Point to the . . .
Understand: Understand the meaning, translation, interpolation, and interpretation of instructions and problems.	comprehend, convert, defend, distinguish, estimate, explain, extend, generalize, give examples, infer, interpret, paraphrase, predict, rewrite, summarize, translate	Tell me in your own words . . . What does it mean . . . Give me an example of . . . Describe what . . . Illustrate the part of the story that . . . Make a map of . . . What is the main idea of . . .
Apply: Use a concept in a new situation or unprompted use of an abstraction.	apply, change, compute, construct, demonstrate, discover, manipulate, modify, operate, predict, prepare, produce, relate, show, solve, use	What would happen to you if . . . Would you have done the same as . . . If you were there, would you . . . How would you solve the problem . . . In the library, find information about . . .
Analyze: Separate material or concepts into component parts so that its organizational structure may be understood.	analyze, break down, compare, contrast, diagram, deconstruct, differentiate, discriminate, distinguish, identify, illustrate, infer, outline, relate, select, separate	What things would you have used . . . What other ways could . . . What things are similar/different? What part of this story was the most exciting? What things couldn't have happened in real life? What kind of person is . . . What caused _____ to act the way he/she did?
Evaluate: Make judgments about the value of ideas or materials.	appraise, compare, conclude, contrast, criticize, critique, defend, describe, discriminate, evaluate, explain, interpret, justify, relate, summarize, support	Would you recommend this book? Why or why not? Select the best . . . Why is it the best? What do you think will happen to . . . Why do you think that? Could this story really have happened? Which character would you most like to meet? Was _____ good or bad? Why? Did you like the story? Why?
Create: Build a structure or pattern from diverse elements. Put parts together to form a whole, with emphasis on creating a new meaning or structure.	categorize, combine, compile, compose, create, devise, design, explain, generate, modify, organize, plan, rearrange, reconstruct, relate, reorganize, revise, rewrite, summarize, tell, write	What would it be like if . . . What would it be like to live . . . Design a . . . Pretend you are a . . . What would have happened if . . . Why/why not? Use your imagination to draw a picture of . . . Add a new item on your own . . . Tell/write a different ending . . .

This process allows the teacher to check for understanding twice—as students create their questions and when they play the game.

Second grade teacher Heather Jennison also uses Bloom's taxonomy in her planning. For example, during her interactive read-aloud of *Nana Upstairs and Nana Downstairs* (dePaola, 1973), Ms. Jennison prepared the following questions:

Remember: What were the names Tommy used for his grandmother and great-grandmother?

Understand: How did Tommy feel when he went to visit them each Sunday?

Apply: What would you have said to Tommy's older brother when he called Nana Upstairs "a witch"?

Analyze: How were Nana Upstairs and Nana Downstairs alike? Different?

Evaluate: Did you like this story? Why or why not? Use evidence from the text to support your answer.

Create: Add a new last page to the book. What might the two grandmothers say to the adult Tommy when he looks at the stars to remember them?

While Bloom's taxonomy provides us with a way of organizing questions, teachers can structure interesting questions in other ways. For example, Webb's (2007) depth of knowledge framework allows teachers to determine the amount of content knowledge needed by students. In this framework, there are four levels: (1) recall and reproduction, (2) skills and concepts, (3) short-term strategic thinking, and (4) extended thinking.

During recall and reproduction (level 1), students are involved in basic tasks that require them to recall information and/or reproduce knowledge/skills. The skills and concepts level (2) requires students to estimate, summarize, compare and contrast, describe or explain, or convert information. Often, this level requires that students explain how or why they used the skill or concept. During strategic thinking, level 3, students are asked to solve complex problems, predict outcomes, or analyze data. Typically, they have to use information from multiple sources or disciplines to complete tasks at this level. At level 4, extended thinking, students must employ strategic thinking to solve problems. Figure 3.2 contains a number of question stems aligned with Webb's depth of knowledge. Note that level 4 involves a project or writing task, rather than a question.

FIGURE 3.2	Question Stems for Webb's Depth of Knowledge

DOK 1

- Can you recall_____?
- When did ____ happen?
- Who was ____?
- How can you recognize____?
- What is____?
- How can you find the meaning of ____?
- Can you recall____?
- Can you select ____?
- How would you write___?
- What might you include on a list about___?
- Who discovered ___?
- What is the formula for___?
- Can you identify___?
- How would you describe___?

DOK 2

- Can you explain how ____ affected ____?
- How would you apply what you learned to develop ____?
- How would you compare ____? Contrast____?
- How would you classify____?
- How are ____ alike? Different?
- How would you classify the type of____?
- What can you say about____?
- How would you summarize____?
- What steps are needed to edit___?
- When would you use an outline to ___?
- How would you estimate___?
- How could you organize___?
- What would you use to classify___?
- What do you notice about___?

DOK 3

- How is ____ related to ____?
- What conclusions can you draw _____?
- How would you adapt ____ to create a different ____?
- How would you test ____?
- Can you predict the outcome if ____?
- What is the best answer? Why?
- What conclusion can be drawn from these three texts?
- What is your interpretation of this text? Support your rationale.
- How would you describe the sequence of ____?
- What facts would you select to support ____?
- Can you elaborate on the reason ____?
- What would happen if___?
- Can you formulate a theory for___?
- How would you test ___?
- Can you elaborate on the reason___?

DOK 4

- Write a thesis, drawing conclusions from multiple sources.
- Design and conduct an experiment.
- Gather information to develop alternative explanations for the results of an experiment.
- Write a research paper on a topic.
- Apply information from one text to another text to develop a persuasive argument.
- What information can you gather to support your idea about___?
- DOK 4 would most likely be the writing of a research paper or applying information from one text to another text to develop a persuasive argument.
- DOK 4 requires time for extended thinking.

Source: Myra Collins; mcollins@truman.edu.

For example, in Pam Day's culinary arts class, the students were asked a number of questions representing different levels of knowledge that their teacher expected. She started with a request for her students: "Please write as many keywords related to stir fry preparation you can think of in your journals." When they had finished this, Ms. Day asked, "Can you create a flow chart describing the steps in this cooking method?" Both of these tasks were level 1, recall and reproduction, and her students performed well on the tasks.

The following day, Ms. Day asked her students demonstrate various skills in front of the class. For example, she asked Andrew to julienne carrots and Heather to sauté mushrooms. These are examples of level 2 knowledge, appropriate for her content. Each student was required to demonstrate a skill or strategy, drawing on vocabulary knowledge. They were also asked, as they were waiting their turn, to engage in a more complex task. They had to respond to the questions "What is the role of stirring for different ingredients in a stir fry?" and "Can you create a set of rules that apply to this cooking method?" This allowed Ms. Day to determine areas of needed additional instruction and groups of students who had developed strong understanding of the content.

In addition to general frameworks for generating questions to check for understanding, there is a specific type of question that requires evidence from a text students are reading. These text-dependent questions can only be answered by carefully analyzing the text. These are useful when teachers want to ensure that students deeply understand the texts that they have read. There are six types of questions (Fisher & Frey, 2013): general understanding, key details, vocabulary and text structure, author's craft and purpose, inferences, and opinion, argument and intertextual connections. For each question type, we will provide an example from Marisol Thayre's class of 11th graders as they studied the forward of *The Picture of Dorian Grey* (Wilde, 1891/1993) in advance of her shared reading and their investigation of the text.

General understanding. These questions focus on the big ideas in, or the gist of, the text. They encourage readers to think about the author's main message or the important lessons. These questions can also focus on the sequence of events. Ms. Thayre's students were asked, "What is the purpose of this preface?" and "What is Wilde's attitude toward art? How do you know?"

Key details. Texts contain details that help readers make sense of the information. These questions often focus on who, what, where, when, why, how much, or how many. They probe important details that are key to understanding the text. Ms. Thayre's students were asked the following: What does an artist *not* do? What is the role of the artist? How will the artist know when he or she is "in accord" with him- or herself?

Vocabulary and text structure. When authors create texts, they select specific words and then organize those words in structures. Questions of this type should explore the meaning of specific words and phrases as well as reasons that the author selected those words. In addition, questions in this category should focus on the structure of the text and the ways in which the structure lead to understanding. While reading the preface, students were introduced to the terms *realism*, *Caliban*, and *romanticism*. Ms. Thayre asked them, "Now that you understand some new terms, what do you make of the following statements:

- 'The nineteenth century dislike of Realism is the rage of Caliban seeing his own face in a glass.'
- 'The nineteenth century dislike of Romanticism is the rage of Caliban not seeing his own face in the glass.'

She also asked, "What is the tone of this piece? What words clue you into Wilde's attitude toward critics?" and "How does the sentence structure and word choice affect the message of the text?"

Author's craft and purpose. As students dig deeper into the text, the questions begin to explore the genre, narration, point of view, and potential bias in the text. These questions allow students to consider the ways in which the author constructed the text and the purpose the author had in doing so. For example, in Ms. Thayre's class, the students discussed "Why does Wilde set up a paradox?"

Inferences. These questions require that students make informed conclusions that are based on evidence from the text and their reasoning about the meaning of the text. As such, they demand evidence from the text but invite students to speculate. For example, in Ms. Thayre's class, students explored, "What is Wilde's reason for including allusions in his preface? Who is the allusion to, and what effect does it have on the text?" and "According to Wilde, should art reflect a lesson or moral message?"

Opinion, argument and intertextual connections. In this final category of text-dependent questions, readers are expected to form an opinion or argument and support their claims with evidence from the text. In addition, they are expected to make connections across texts to deepen their understanding of the text under investigation. For example, in Ms. Thayre's class, students were asked, "What is Wilde's attitude toward art? How do you know?" They also read some of the criticism of his text and were asked, "Given the reception of critics, how does your perception of the preface, which was added after the novel's initial release, change?"

Not all texts deserve the level of scrutiny afforded by text-dependent questions, but some do. When the lesson purpose is to check for deep understanding of a text, these types of questions help teachers determine what students understand and what they still need to learn. Figure 3.3 contains additional sample text-dependent questions. These are based on *The Day the Crayons Quit* (Daywalt, 2013), a picture book for children, and a geology entry from the *U*X*L Encyclopedia of Science*.

Responding When Students Don't Get It

How teachers respond to students' incorrect answers to questions is really important. Simply telling students the answer to a question that they got wrong will not ensure that they understand the information. Instead, it sends a message that they don't really have to think about the questions that the teacher poses, but rather can simply guess and then be told if their thinking is correct or not. Over time, this creates learned helplessness as students become dependent on adults for information and answers. Instead, teachers have to carefully consider how they respond to errors and misconceptions.

As we noted in *Guided Instruction: How to Develop Confident and Successful Learners* (Fisher & Frey, 2010), teachers can use three types of scaffolds to avoid the learned helplessness that has become all too common in schools. These scaffolds are questions, prompts, and cues.

Questions. Sometimes asking students another question will unlock information and clear up confusions. Teachers may rephrase a question or ask a follow-up question. In doing so, they are providing the student additional time to think. They are also providing the student an alternative way to think about the information.

	FIGURE 3.3	Sample text-dependent questions	

Question Type	*The Day the Crayons Quit*	Geology entry from *The U*X*L Encyclopedia of Science*
General understanding	What does each crayon want? What did Duncan find when he took his crayons out of the box one day?	What are the two main branches of geology?
Key details	Why is Blue so short and stubby? For how many years has blue been his favorite color? What are Yellow and Orange arguing about?	What are the four branches of study for physical geologists? What are the two areas of historical geology discussed in the article?
Vocabulary and text structure	The author uses the word "BREAK" near the end of the blue's entry. What does the word "BREAK" mean in the text? How does the structure of the letter allow the reader to gain an understanding of the gray crayon's point of view?	Which terms are associated with the study of physical processes? Which terms are associated with the study of chemical processes? Which terms are utilized in the study of both physical and chemical processes?
Author's craft and purpose	How does each crayon "advocate" for itself? What is the effect of the rhetorical question that concludes Beige Crayon's letter: "when was the last time you saw a kid excited about coloring wheat?"? How is Beige Crayon's argument different stylistically from Pink and Black Crayons'? Why does the author write from different point of views? What effect does that have on the story?	What is the writer's purpose for this article? How does its source support your answer?
Inferences	Which crayons appear sad? How can you tell? Why does Beige state that he is proud of his color but seems jealous of Mr. Brown?	What would not be well understood about the Earth if not for the fields of physical and historical geology?
Opinion, argument and inter-textual connections	Which crayon advocated for itself best? Use textual evidence and your own inferences to support your analysis. Based on your evaluation of the effectiveness of the red crayon's argument, should Duncan stop using the red crayon? Use evidence from the text to support your position.	How does the writer make the case that the branches of physical and historical geology need one another? This article provides a brief overview of the field of geology. Where can you find more detailed information about specific branches of geological study?

Information from this entire chapter can be used to create follow-up questions that serve as a scaffold. For example, if a student were unable to answer a question that required evaluation, the teacher may ask a follow-up question that focuses on comprehension.

Prompts. Another way to scaffold students' understanding is to prompt cognitive or metacognive work. Prompts are designed to cause something to happen in the learner's mind. There are at least four types of prompts, as noted in Figure 3.4. For example, when the student gets the wrong answer from not following the correct order of operations while solving a math problem, the teacher says, "I'm thinking about a mnemonic that we used to remember the order for solving problems."

Cues. A third way to scaffold students' understanding is to shift their attention. Cues are designed to guide students to notice something that they have missed. There are at least four types of cues, as noted in Figure 3.5. As we noted earlier, this may be as simple as asking a student to look back into a text at a graphic or visual that was provided by the author. It may also be a gesture to the word wall or a change in verbal emphasis, focusing on a key word in the statement that the teacher made.

The goal is for questions to provide students with an opportunity to think and the teacher with an opportunity to check for understanding.

Providing Nonverbal Support

In addition to the dialogic support teachers offer in helping their students construct answers, nonverbal cues can promote or discourage learner response. You have probably been asked a question by someone and started to respond, only to find that he or she does not appear to be listening to your reply. The person may be looking over your shoulder or may turn away from you to complete a task. It's likely that you immediately thought, "Now, why did he even bother to ask?" It is also likely that you were not inclined to continue the conversation. This type of interaction occurs in classrooms each day. Busy teachers attempt to multitask, posing a question while distributing papers. Or another student catches the teacher's eye, and she turns her back on the student who is attempting to offer a reply. This is usually inadvertent, yet the effect is the same: "Why did she bother to ask?" Of even more concern, the student may think, "I won't bother to answer again."

FIGURE 3.4	Types of Prompts	
Type of Prompt	**Definition**	**Examples**
Background knowledge	Content that the student already knows, has been taught, or has experienced but has temporarily forgotten or is not using the information correctly	• In a lesson requiring map skills, the social studies teacher says, "Can the legend be used to help you answer this question about Magellan's voyages?" • In an environmental science class, the teacher says, "How can you use what you know about Bernoulli's principle to solve this design problem?"
Process or procedure	Established or generally agreed-upon rules or guidelines are not being followed, and a reminder will help resolve the error or misconception	• When a student is having difficulty locating a term in a dictionary, the teacher says, "I'm thinking about how the guide words feature can be used to find a word quickly." • In an anatomy and physiology unit, the biology teacher says, "Knowing smooth muscle tissue fully contracts and relaxes the entire muscle, how would that affect the blood flow?"
Reflective	Asking students to be metacognitive and think about their thinking, which can then be used to determine next steps or the solution to a problem	• In a math class, the teacher says, "Look again at the answer. Does that seem probable? Think about the estimate you made before you calculated." • When a student is not responding accurately to a writing prompt, the teacher says, "Read the prompt again and break it into sections. Is your response addressing what the prompt is asking?"
Heuristic	Informal problem-solving procedures used to help learners develop their own way to solve problems. They do not have to be the same as others' heuristics, but they do need to work.	• In a math class, the teacher says, "When I have to count a lot of items, I make tally marks. Could that help you to count the responses on the surveys?" • In a video production class, the teacher says, "I can see you're having trouble composing this next shot. Could altering the perspective to a worm's eye view or bird's eye view address your dilemma?"

FIGURE 3.5	Types of Cues	
Type of Cue	**Definition**	**Example**
Visual	A range of graphic hints that guide students' thinking or understanding	• Using a language chart to record student responses • Annotation marks in a written text • Creating a data table in math or science
Verbal	Variations in speech used to draw attention to something specific or verbal attention getters that focus students' thinking	• "This is the part where everything will change for the character" • Reading a student's writing aloud so he can hear the syntactic error he has made • Changing volume or rate of speech to draw attention to a statement
Gestural	Teacher's body movements or motions used to draw attention to something that has been missed	• Pointing to the steps in a set of directions that are written on the board to signal an error a student has made • Raising each finger on the hand while counting items • Lowering both hands at an equal rate while discussing the rate of two falling objects
Environmental	Using the surroundings, and things in the surroundings, to influence students' understanding	• Shifting a reference book into a student's view to remind her that the resource will assist her in resolving a problem • Drawing a language chart closer to the table to shift the student's attention to the information on it • Changing a geometric shape's orientation in order for the student to recognize it

Nonverbal cues convey a tone of respect for the respondent and encourage the target student and others to continue to participate. Kindsvatter, Wilen, and Ishler (1996) identify seven components of listening that teachers can and should use to communicate with students that their ideas and participation are valued. They suggest that these seven components indicate to students that the adult is interested and that the student is worthy of attention:

Eye contact. Look directly at the speaker and maintain eye contact.
Facial expressions. Use a variety of appropriate facial expressions, such as smiling or demonstrating surprise or excitement.

Body posture. Use gestures such as hand signals; maintain body posture that signifies openness to students' ideas.

Physical distance. Adjust your position in the classroom according to your condition of instruction; for example, move closer to a student who is speaking (or to a student who is less engaged).

Silence. Be quiet while a student is speaking; don't interrupt; honor wait times after a student stops speaking.

Verbal acknowledgments. Use brief, appropriate verbal acknowledgments such as "Go ahead," "Yes," or "I understand."

Subsummaries. Restate or paraphrase the main ideas presented by students during lengthy discussions.

These simple techniques convey respect for the speaker and provide the questioner with the opportunity to analyze the response and make decisions about scaffolds and feedback. By attending to the respondent and the response, the answer can be used as a means to check for understanding. A distracted teacher is incapable of engaging in anything beyond a superficial awareness of whether the answer was correct or incorrect.

Instructional Practices That Promote Participation

In addition to creating quality questions and monitoring nonverbal behavior, there are a number of instructional practices that teachers can use to increase participation and engagement in the classroom. The following strategies are especially useful in the area of questioning and may also apply to other methods of checking for understanding.

Response Cards

Response cards are index cards, signs, dry-erase boards, magnetic boards, or other items that are simultaneously held up by all students in class to indicate their response to a question or problem presented by the teacher. By using response cards, the teacher can easily note the responses of individual students while teaching the whole group. Additionally, response cards allow for participation by the whole class and not just a few students who raise their hands to respond (Heward et al., 1996).

While there are a number of examples of response cards, there are basically two types: preprinted and write-on cards. Preprinted cards already have responses on them; write-on cards allow students to indicate their responses in real time. There are specific reasons to use each.

When Dana Nielsen wanted her 1st grade students to learn to use response cards, she first provided each student with two preprinted index cards that read "yes" and "no." Then, she introduced the picture book *George and Martha* (Marshall, 1974). Looking at the cover, she asked her students, "Are these dogs?" Several hands shot up; Alicia shouted out, "NO!" Ms. Nielsen paused and looked at the class. She reminded them that they should use their response cards and asked the question again. This time, all of the students held up their "no" cards. Ms. Nielsen then asked, "Is this story a real story? Do you think it could really happen?" Most of the class held up their "no" cards, but four held up "yes" cards. Ms. Nielsen said, "Hmm, I wonder if these animals really are friends and would wear clothes like this." She then pointed to the name of the author, read it aloud, and asked, "Is this the name of the author?" All of the "yes" cards were displayed. Ms. Nielsen was quite pleased to see this as she had been focusing her instruction on identifying title and author information. As she read the book, she paused periodically to ask questions. At one point she asked, "Do you think Martha likes split pea soup?" About half of the "yes" cards went up. She asked Jeremy why he held up his "yes" card, and he answered, "Because she likes to make it. See right there? She likes to cook that." Ms. Nielsen then asked Brianna why she held up her "no" card. Brianna replied, "Yuck, peas! She can't like that." The use of these preprinted response cards ensured that all of the students remained focused on the content of the text and allowed Ms. Nielsen to check her students' understanding of the information on a regular basis.

Mr. Hernandez uses response cards with his 3rd grade students during their word study lessons. He purchased tile board (used in shower stalls) from his local hardware store and had it cut into 12-inch squares. These work great with dry-erase pens as low-cost personal write-on, wipe-off boards.

Mr. Hernandez displayed a bunch of scrambled letters (*d, s, i, a, n, u, o, r*) on the projector. Students were asked to write three-letter words using these letters and hold up their boards. The range of student responses included *nor, our, sin, sun, son, and, run, ran,* and *dor.* (Mr. Hernandez noted that Tony had incorrectly spelled *door* as *dor.*) Then Mr. Hernandez asked students to create four-letter words using these letters. The range of words now included *rain, dino, sour, sins, said, raid,* and so on. These write-on response cards allowed Mr. Hernandez to check his students' understanding of word study while his students identified longer and longer words from the letters that eventually formed the word *dinosaur.*

Physics teacher Tom Jensen uses preprinted response cards that read "potential energy" and "kinetic energy" as part of his instruction on matter and motion. Using an LCD projector to display images on the screen, Mr. Jensen asked his students to identify if the energy being displayed was potential or kinetic. In response to a slide showing a stretched rubber band, all of the students held up their "potential energy" cards. To a slide of a pitcher throwing a baseball, all but two students held up their "kinetic energy" cards. Additional slides focused on roller coasters, a professional runner, a glass of water at the edge of a dinner table, and so on. Several slides later, the image of a massive waterfall was displayed. The majority of the students held up their "kinetic energy" cards. Mr. Jensen asked Antony why he held up his "potential energy" card. Antony responded, "I see more potential energy. Look at all that water ready to go over the edge. The majority of the information in this picture suggests potential; only a small amount of the water is really kinetic at any one time." Mr. Jensen's use of response cards allowed him to check his students' understanding of the key ideas they were learning. These cards also allowed him to note areas of weakness or misconceptions that he could address in his subsequent small-group guided instruction.

Hand Signals

Hand signals are often used as a classroom management tool. For example, Wong and Wong (2005) suggest a classroom procedure called "Give Me Five" in which students are taught specific behavioral expectations for each of the numbers 5, 4, 3, 2, and 1 as the teacher counts down on his or her fingers. Hand signals have also been successfully used to ensure that students with ADD/ADHD or behavioral disabilities get immediate and private feedback from their teachers (and possibly trusted peers) regarding their performance.

Students can also use hand signals to indicate their understanding of content information. Similar to response cards, hand signals require engagement from the whole group and allow the teacher to check for understanding in large groups of students.

In her kindergarten classroom, Donna Kim uses "thumbs up" to check her students' understanding of instructions and information. Her students know how to display the following signals:

Thumbs up: "I understand _____ and can explain it."
Thumbs sideways: "I'm not completely sure about _____."
Thumbs down: "I do not yet understand _____."

At one point, Ms. Kim used the "thumbs up" procedure to determine which of her students needed additional assistance in their journal writing. The task involved writing at least two follow-up sentences and drawing an illustration of kangaroos based on a shared reading and interactive writing lesson the class had just completed. Ms. Kim reminded her students that the sentences needed to be informational and not fiction. She then said, "Thumbs up?" Several students immediately put their thumbs up and were dismissed to their tables. A few students had their thumbs sideways, and three had their thumbs down. Ms. Kim started with Creshena, who had her thumb sideways. Creshena asked, "You mean it could really happen, right?" Ms. Kim replied, "Yes, informational—not fiction or pretend." When all of the students who had their thumbs sideways had their questions answered and were sitting at their desks writing and illustrating, Ms. Kim focused on the students with their thumbs down. She reviewed the shared reading text, thinking aloud about the range of possible sentences that her students might want to write.

Using this procedure, Ms. Kim was able to allocate instructional time to students who really needed additional support to be successful. In addition, her ability to check for understanding ensured that her students were successful in completing the task at hand.

Seventh grade pre-algebra teacher Tara Jacobsen also uses hand signals to check her students' understanding. As she models the solutions to word problems, she asks her students to hold up fingers based on how well they understand each step along the way. Five fingers means that you have a deep understanding and can explain this step or idea to others in the class; one finger means that you have no idea what just happened. Two to four fingers indicate varying levels of understanding.

As Ms. Jacobsen worked out a problem on the document camera, she shared her thinking and checked for understanding regularly. The problem read as follows:

An 800-seat multiplex is divided into three theaters. There are 270 seats in Theater 1, and there are 150 more seats in Theater 2 than in Theater 3. How many seats are in Theater 2?

Ms. Jacobsen: Okay, so my total has to equal 800; that's all the seats we have in the whole thing. Fingers?

All hands are showing five fingers.

Ms. Jacobsen: I know that there are 270 seats exactly in Theater 1. Fingers?

All hands show five fingers.

Ms. Jacobsen: Well, that's not a lot of help yet. We need to know how many are in Theater 2. There are 150 more seats in Theater 2 than in Theater 3. Thoughts?

Almost all hands show five fingers; three students show three or four.

Ms. Jacobsen: Let me think about this again. [She underlines "150 more seats."] There are 150 more seats in Theater 2 than in Theater 3. So I know that Theater 2 has to be bigger than Theater 3 by 150 seats. Responses?

All hands again show five fingers.

Ms. Jacobsen: So, if Theater 3 is represented as x, then Theater 2 can be represented as $x + 150$, because there are 150 more seats in Theater 2 than 3. Fingers?

All hands show five fingers.

Ms. Jacobsen: I know that all three theaters have to add up to 800. T1 + T2 + T3 = 800. Reactions?

All hands show five fingers.

Ms. Jacobsen: I know that T1 is 270. Fingers?

All hands show five fingers.

Ms. Jacobsen: I know that T2 is $x + 150$. Thoughts?

All hands show five fingers.

Ms. Jacobsen: I know that T3 is x. Fingers?

All hands show five fingers.

Ms. Jacobsen: So, my formula is $270 + (x + 150) + x = 800$. Do you agree?

All hands show five fingers.

Ms. Jacobsen: So I can add like terms: $420 + 2x = 800$. Fingers?

Many hands show four fingers; several students show one or two.

Ms. Jacobsen: Oh, so here's the problem. We need to think about adding like terms. Talk with your partner and explain how like terms are added. [Students start talking with one another.]

Ms. Jacobsen: Here's how I did this. I added the numbers together: $270 + 150 = 420$. There isn't a multiplication sign to confuse us; we can just add. Fingers?

All hands show five fingers.

Ms. Jacobsen: Then I added x and x together. Is this what you talked about with your partners? Mikel, what did your partner tell you?

Mikel: She said that the two unknowns could be added because they were both the same kind—x.

Ms. Jacobsen: Right. Are you all thinking that? Do you agree?

All hands show five fingers.

Ms. Jacobsen: Now, I just need to solve for the x. That's the simple part, right? So my answer is 190. Thoughts?

All hands show five fingers.

Ms. Jacobsen: But let's check our variables. We let x = Theater 3. Remember that we were asked to find out how many seats were in Theater 2. So we have to return to our variables and remember that Theater 2 is $x + 150$. So Theater 2, my answer, is 340. Fingers?

All hands show five fingers.

Ms. Jacobsen: Let's check to see if this works. We know that Theater 1 has 270 seats. We learned that Theater 3 has 190. We know that Theater 2, from our addition, has 340 seats. So let's add those together. Do we get 800? Fingers?

All hands show five fingers.

The use of hand signals allowed Ms. Jacobsen to identify the places where her students did not understand the math content so that she could reteach this information on the spot. Checking for understanding as she modeled the solution to the word problem increased the likelihood that her students could use this information to solve similar problems in small groups and eventually on their own.

Audience Response Systems

New technologies have provided teachers with unique opportunities for checking for understanding. For example, Audience Response Systems (ARS)—handheld devices (e.g., remote controls or "clickers") that allow each learner to respond to questions individually—enable teachers to gather students' responses to interactive questions in real time. Most systems of this type are integrated into software programs such as PowerPoint so that the responses are aggregated and displayed immediately.

Tom Hayden uses an ARS to engage his middle school science students during their unit of study on cells. At one point, he asked the following question:

What is the function of the cell membrane?

A. Cytoplasm
B. Chloroplasts
C. Cell wall

Students quickly entered their responses on their handheld devices. Over 90 percent of the students had this answer correct. Mr. Hayden congratulated his students and quickly summarized the answer: "Yep, cytoplasm. Both animal and plant cells have cytoplasm. You'll recall that cytoplasm is jellylike material that fills cells."

Pleased that his students knew this, he continued to ask questions, provide answers, and integrate brief lecture points into this experience with his students. They remained engaged, waiting for opportunities to demonstrate their knowledge of science. This changed when he asked the following question:

What is the function of the cell membrane?

A. To control which substances move in and out of the cell
B. To help the cell maintain a firm shape
C. To make food for the cell
D. All of the above

More than half of the students selected D; the other half were spread across answers A, B, and C. Mr. Hayden was clearly surprised. "Wow!" he responded. "That membrane really caught us! Why does the cell have a membrane? Let's look at this illustration again. [He turned on the document camera and displayed a diagram of a cell.] Tell your partner how the cell maintains its shape. [He paused while students talked.] Ah, yes, I'm hearing the answer all around. The cell *wall* helps the cell maintain its shape. So B can't be correct. Try again, everyone. [Students reentered their responses on the handheld devices.] Oh, I'm glad to see no one selected B and only a few people selected C, but lots of you selected D. How could that be if we just determined that B can't be correct? If B isn't correct, then D can't be your answer. Let's review some test-taking skills. . . ."

Using technology, questions, and systems for checking for understanding, Mr. Hayden was able to challenge his students' knowledge and misconceptions and provide them with a strong foundation in understanding the physical and biological world.

ReQuest

ReQuest, or reciprocal questioning (Manzo, 1969), was designed to teach students to ask and answer questions as they read. We know that good readers engage in questioning as they read, and teaching students to do this will improve their comprehension. In fact, simply thinking about questions while reading improves comprehension, whether the questions are "question-the-author" questions, "question–answer relationship" questions, or dense questions (Beck, McKeown, Hamilton, & Kucan, 1997; Raphael, Highfield, & Au, 2006).

The original version of ReQuest requires that the teacher lead the whole class in silently reading a segment of text. Students then ask questions of the teacher about the content of the section of text they read. Next, the students and the teacher change roles. They all read the next section of the text silently. When they finish the second segment of text, the teacher questions the students. They take turns back and forth alternating between questioning and responding. As the ReQuest process continues, students learn to imitate the teacher's questioning behavior.

Physics teacher Vince Andrews uses ReQuest in his classroom on a weekly basis. He starts each term modeling ReQuest with his students as outlined above. Over time, he transfers the responsibility totally to his students. They work in pairs, taking turns responding and questioning as they read complex pieces of text. In one instance, students focused on an online text about amusement park physics (www.learner.org/exhibits/parkphysics/index.html). After reading, pairs of students asked and answered questions about roller coasters, how they work, how mass has an impact on the ride, and so on. After reading the section "Wooden or Steel Coaster: Does It Make a Difference?" one student, Violet, asked the following questions:

- What role does the construction material play in the ride?
- What are the advantages and disadvantages of each type of coaster?
- Which would you rather ride and why?
- Which do you think is safer and why?

Socratic Seminar

The Greek philosopher and teacher Socrates (ca. 470–399 BCE) was convinced that the way to gain reliable knowledge was through the practice of disciplined conversation. He called this method *dialectic,* which means the art or practice of examining opinions or ideas logically, often by the method of question and answer, so as to determine their validity.

Educators have developed the Socratic seminar as a way of engaging a group of learners in a conversation and series of questions. There are a number of considerations to address when conducting Socratic seminars, including the text, the question, the leader, and the participants.

The text. Socratic seminar texts should be selected for their ability to engage students in discussion. The text should be rich enough to ensure that readers will ask and answer questions for themselves. Both narrative and informational texts can be used in Socratic seminars. The most important thing is that the text can capture the imagination of the group.

The question. A Socratic seminar begins with a question posed by the leader. As students develop their expertise in Socratic seminars, they will begin asking questions themselves. The question should have no right answer. Instead, the question should reflect authentic wonder and interest. A good opening question requires that students return to the text to think, search, evaluate, wonder, or infer. Responses to the opening question should generate new questions, leading to new responses and still more questions. In a Socratic seminar, inquiry is natural and continuous.

The leader. In a Socratic seminar, the leader serves as both participant in and facilitator of the discussion. The seminar leader demonstrates "habits of mind" (see

Costa & Kallick, 2000) that lead to a reflective and thoughtful exploration of the ideas presented in the text and referenced in the discussion. In addition to this facilitator role, the leader is also a seminar participant. As such, the leader actively takes part in the group's examination of the text. Naturally, the leader must know the text well enough to anticipate misconceptions and misunderstandings, various interpretations, reader responses, and issues that may invoke strong emotions. At the same time, the leader must trust the process and allow the group to come to its own understanding of the text and the ideas represented in the text.

The participants. In a Socratic seminar, participants are responsible for the quality of the seminar and discussion. Good seminars result when participants study the text in advance; listen actively; share their ideas, opinions, and questions; and search for evidence in the text to support their ideas. Over time, participants realize that the leader is not expecting "right answers" to the questions that are asked, but instead is hoping to get students to think out loud as they discover the excitement of exploring important issues through shared inquiry.

Tips for Success

Questioning is a powerful tool that teachers can use to engage students in authentic learning. Questioning is also an excellent way for teachers to check for understanding. There are a number of effective approaches to questioning, both at the individual level and at the classroom level. However, questions can be ineffective when they are not thoughtfully planned or when a teacher's nonverbal behavior indicates lack of interest in the responses or the individual responding.

Some tips to consider as you create questions to check for understanding include the following:

• Plan questions in advance based on the lesson purpose and intended learning outcomes. Check to make sure that the questions represent a range of cognitive tasks.
• Listen carefully to students' responses to the questions to determine if additional instruction is needed. Pay attention to your own nonverbal behavior and the messages it might send to students.

• Plan scaffolds in advance based on the types of errors that students are likely to make. Check to make sure that additional questions, prompts, and cues provide scaffolding for students.

• Use instructional practices that allow for many students to participate simultaneously. Increasing the number of students who participate increases engagement and provides additional opportunities to check for understanding and to catch students before they fall.

4

Using Writing to Check
for Understanding

Writing clarifies thinking. For that matter, writing *is* thinking. Analyzing student writing is a great way for teachers to determine what their students know. In this chapter, we explore the use of writing to check for understanding. We consider various writing prompts and how teachers can use the writing they receive from students to determine the next steps to take in their instruction. This chapter focuses on the use of writing across the curriculum as an assessment tool and not the teaching of writing for writing's sake. Elbow (1994) describes two purposes for writing:

> It is helpful to distinguish between two very different goals for writing. The normal and conventional goal is writing to demonstrate learning: for this goal the writing should be good—it should be clear and, well . . . right. It is high stakes writing. We all know and value this kind of writing so I don't need to argue for it here, but let me give one more reason why it's important: if we don't ask students to demonstrate their learning in essays and essay exams, we are likely to grade unfairly because of being misled about how much they have learned in our course. Students often seem to know things on short-answer or multiple-choice tests that they don't really understand.
>
> But there is another important kind of writing that is less commonly used and valued, and so I want to stress it here: writing for learning. This is

low stakes writing. The goal isn't so much good writing as coming to learn, understand, remember and figure out what you don't yet know. Even though low stakes writing-to-learn is not always good as writing, it is particularly effective at promoting learning and involvement in course material, and it is much easier on teachers—especially those who aren't writing teachers. (p. 1)

It is Elbow's second purpose that is the focus of this chapter. Writing to learn is a powerful tool for students. It helps them clarify their thinking and their understanding. Once students have an opportunity to clarify their thinking and understanding, teachers can use these permanent products to determine misconceptions, errors in thinking, and additional needed instruction. To elicit this kind of student thinking, teachers must design prompts that cause students to explore a topic or issue. To develop these prompts, teachers and students should be clear about the appropriate text types or genres to be used.

Text Types and Genres

There are three general text types that comprise most writing that is used to check for understanding: narrative, informational/explanatory, and opinion/argument.

- **Narratives** convey a real or imagined experience over a period of time. These often include people and use dialogue.
- **Informational/explanatory texts** are used to explain a phenomenon, concept, or procedure.
- **Opinions/arguments** are constructed to persuade a reader using evidence, logic, and rhetoric.

These text types are expressed in a variety of fiction and nonfiction genres. Figure 4.1 includes genres associated with each of the three text types.

Too often, emphasis is on the form of the piece. Young children develop step-by-step instructions for making a peanut butter and jelly sandwich, with each point in the process numbered in sequence. Older students are instructed to state their position and address counterarguments in order to write a successful argument. It is less common to analyze the content of the writing itself. For example, what does the informative piece reveal about what the 1st grade student knows and does not

FIGURE 4.1	Text Types and Associated Genres
Text type	**Genre**
Narrative	• Stories • Biographies and autobiographies • Testimonials • First-person accounts • Friendly letter • Anecdotes • Memoirs
Informational/Explanatory	• Literary analysis • Summaries • Reports • Précis • Instructions • Memos
Opinion/Argument	• Argumentative essay • Editorials and opinion pieces • Scientific research • Primary and secondary source analysis

know regarding sandwich assembly? How pertinent is the information cited by the 7th grader regarding the claims made in support of a position?

Perhaps the most well publicized example of this phenomenon was the analysis of the results of the first administration of the SAT writing test. Massachusetts Institute of Technology professor Les Perelman analyzed the length and content of the 54 anchor papers, graded essays, and samples released by the publisher of the test and discovered a strong correlation between length and score. "I have never found a quantifiable predictor in 25 years of grading that was anywhere near as strong as this one," he reported. "If you just graded them based on length without ever reading them, you'd be right over 90 percent of the time" (in Winerip, 2005). According to the *New York Times* article, Perelman reported that the scoring manual for the test stated that factual errors were not to be factored into the score for the essay (Winerip, 2005).

Using writing to check for understanding means looking at how the form and the content interact. Since writing is thinking, the message and the way the message is conveyed are interrelated. The execution of the form should support the information being communicated. In this way, the ability to narrate, to inform, or to argue becomes a mechanism for looking at the ways in which students understand.

Misuses of Writing in the Classroom

Student writing can provide a rich resource for determining what students know and don't know, and it can lead to future instructional decisions, but none of this can occur when writing is ignored or inconsistently assessed. In some cases, the writing is viewed as the end product, with no thought given to the instruction that should follow. Instead, the writing is graded and students never have the opportunity to extend their thinking because the writing is never revisited. Rather than opportunities for writing popping up throughout a unit, they occur only near the end. Even when writing is interspersed throughout a unit, students and their teachers may not look across a series of writing episodes to gauge the learning progression.

Another misuse of writing assignments is when the feedback is not adequately aligned to the task. For example, students are asked to provide evidence to support claims, but are not given feedback about the whether the evidence is credible and substantial. Perhaps the most common misuse is in focusing feedback on the conventions and mechanics of writing, with little attention to content. Spelling and grammatical errors are dutifully noted, but feedback about the ideas, reasoning, and use of evidence are lacking. This is not to say that conventions and mechanics should be ignored. In fact, if the teaching point was about using dependent clauses correctly, then of course the feedback should be about this. But don't forget the writing task itself, which undoubtedly was about content, not clauses. The content itself should not be ignored at the expense of the mechanics.

In some places, writing is used as a consequence for problematic behavior. Writing should not be used to address a needed correction in behavior. When a teacher requires that a student write an explanation about why she was late or why he did not complete his homework, there is a telegraphed message to students that writing is neither fun nor something that requires thinking. Furthermore, this type of writing does not allow the teacher to check for understanding.

Writing Strategies to Check for Understanding

You can use writing in a number of ways to check for understanding. During language arts instruction, writing can be used to determine the next steps for instruction in topics such as grammar, spelling, and comprehension. During content-area instruction, student writing can be used to determine what students know, what they still need to know, and what they are confused about. As Kuhrt and Farris (1990) remind us, "the upper reaches of Bloom's taxonomy could not be reached without the use of some form of writing" (p. 437).

Interactive Writing

Interactive writing allows students to share the pen with the teacher. This strategy can be used with individual students, small groups, or the whole class. After agreeing on a message orally, students take turns writing on the dry-erase board or on chart paper. The idea is that interactive writing flows "from ideas, to spoken words, to printed messages" (Clay, 2001, p. 27). The procedures are fairly straightforward. First, the writers discuss a topic and agree on a message. This takes ideas and moves them into spoken words. The teacher then asks students to come write a section of the message. This can be a letter, a word, or a phrase. As each writer finishes, the whole group reads the message aloud, both the part already written and the part still in their minds. While each student writes, the teacher provides related instruction to the rest of the class. For example, in a phonics lesson, if a given writer were writing the word *string,* the teacher may ask members of the class to identify other words with the onset pattern *str-* (such as *strong, strain,* or *stripe*). These lessons extend students' thinking about print and their understandings of the conventions of language and are based on errors, misunderstandings, or next steps for learning that the teacher has identified through checking for understanding (Gibson, 2008; McCarrier, Pinnell, & Fountas, 2000).

The 2nd graders in Rebecca Fieler's class used interactive writing to create a friendly letter using a narrative text type. They had just finished listening to and reading *The Jazz Fly* (Gollub, 2000). As a class, they discussed composing a friendly letter (genre) and decided that they would write to the author and tell him that they enjoyed his singing on the CD that accompanies the book, his illustrations, and the funny story about the fly that uses the sounds of other animals to make music for the bugs. One at a time, students wrote on a piece of chart paper.

When Justin approached the chart paper, instead of the word *really,* he wrote *willy.* Ms. Fieler took note of this misunderstanding and responded this way:

Ms. Fieler: Justin, let's take a second look at this word. It's *really.* Let's say the whole sentence again as a class. *We really like your book.* Justin, do you want to change anything?

Justin: Oh, yeah. [Justin returns to the chart paper and uses a large strip of correction tape to change the word to *Reely.*]

Ms. Fieler: Interesting. I know that there are two ways to spell the root word: *real* and *reel.* [Ms. Fieler writes both on the dry-erase board.] *Real* means true or accurate. *Reel* is like a fishing reel or movie projector reel. Which one do you think would be the correct one for *really*?

Justin [hitting his head with his hand]: Oops, I got the wrong one. It should be *real.* [Justin uses the correction tape to change *Reely* to *Realy.*]

Ms. Fieler: Oh, now I see. But when I say "real-ly," do you hear one or two syllables?

Justin: Two. Yeah, two.

Ms. Fieler: Let's think about what we know about double consonants.

Justin: [He pauses.] There's a vowel close by. [Ms. Fieler had taught this mnemonic a few weeks earlier.]

Ms. Fieler: That's right! So what do you want to add?

Justin: Yeah, so it should be *really.* [Justin adds the second *l* to the word.]

Ms. Fieler: You're amazing. I really appreciate your thinking through this word with me. I bet the class appreciates your hard work in making our letter correct. I see how you wrote your word below with an editor's mark. I also see that you used a capital letter to start the word. I think I know why you did that. Is it because it's a new line?

Justin: Yeah. But the word goes there [he points to the space where the incorrect version was], so it should be a small letter. [Justin uses the correction tape to change the letter *R* to lowercase.]

Ms. Fieler: Excellent. Who wants to add the next word in our friendly letter to Mr. Gollub? [Several hands go up.] Andrea, come on up.

Interactive writing can also be used with older students (Fisher & Frey, 2007). While younger students are often eager to jump out of their seats and participate in writing events, older students are usually more reluctant. When teachers use interactive writing to check for understanding with older students, they need to have firmly established routines and the trust of their students.

Brooke Silva is a 9th grade English teacher who uses interactive writing in her classroom. She regularly meets with small groups of students based on instructional needs that she has identified in their writing. Amalee, Amor, Jorge, and Tien regularly forget the plural -s and possessive -s in their speaking and writing. During their small-group meetings, Ms. Silva discusses current events with her students, and they summarize the discussions through interactive writing. Ms. Silva pays close attention to the plural and possessive endings as her instructional focus. During one of the small-group meetings, students were discussing North Korea's test of nuclear missiles. The group agreed on several opinion/argument sentences to write, including, "Testing missiles is dangerous and may not be in the world's best interest." Tien was the first to write, and he correctly wrote the word *Testing* with a capital letter. As he was writing, Ms. Silva asked her students to think about the various uses of the word *testing* and provided a lesson on words that have multiple meanings. Amalee wrote the next word, *missile,* leaving off the plural -s. Ms. Silva paused in the small-group discussion and asked the group to repeat the sentence. She then asked them if the word *missile* was possessive ("Does the missile own something?") or if it was plural ("Is there more than one?"). Through her small-group interactive writing, Ms. Silva is able to determine what her students know about the content—in this case word analysis and vocabulary—and what she still needs to teach, practice, and reinforce.

Read-Write-Pair-Share

Building on the Think-Pair-Share strategy discussed in Chapter 2, Read-Write-Pair-Share focuses on print-based literacy skills while still encouraging partners to discuss and make meaning of content. The procedure is fairly straightforward. Students read (or view, in the case of videos) the material, write in response to this information, engage in a partner conversation about what they've read and written, and then share their ideas with the whole class. This allows the teacher to check for understanding. For example, the written responses may be a source of information about what students already know or misunderstand. Similarly, listening in on the partner conversations provides the teacher with valuable information about students' thinking.

Students in a 10th grade world history class engaged in Read-Write-Pair-Share in their analysis of the poem "In Flanders Field" (Mcrae, 1915). After reading the poem, students wrote about their initial understanding using an opinion/argument text type, first interpreting the main message and providing evidence to support their claims. Students then shared their writing with partners before transitioning to a class discussion of the piece. The teacher had students reread their initial writing, then draw a line to signal their second entry after the discussion (see Monique's writing in Figure 4.2). The teacher commented that he was most interested in

FIGURE 4.2	Quickwrite

QUICK Write:

• The author was describing a battle that had happend in Flanders Field. He also talked about those who died in the fight and how they don't want the others to give up.

• I think the author supports war because he encourages it,

" To you from failing hands we throw the torch "

I believe that the message of the poem was that the fallen soldiers wanted the others to continue in their footsteps. How they want them to continue the battle, and if they don't the fallen won't be put at rest/peace. "To you from failing hands we throw the torch." "If ye break faith with us who die, we shall not sleep."

looking for the shift in thinking that had transpired over the course of the lesson. In Monique's case, she initially focused what she perceived as the author's support for the war. Only through the discussion did she realize that the poet was giving voice to the dead soldiers, who were encouraging their comrades to fight on in order to make their deaths meaningful.

Summary and Précis Writing

Summary writing is a valuable tool for checking for understanding because it provides the teacher with insight into how learners condense information. It is analogous to retelling (see Chapter 2) and serves as a way for students to demonstrate their ability to recapitulate what they have read, viewed, or done. There is evidence that the act of summarizing new knowledge in written form can lead to higher levels of understanding. Radmacher and Latosi-Sawin (1995) found that college students who wrote summaries as part of their course scored an average of 8 percent higher on their final exam, compared to students who did not write summaries.

The most common form of summary writing is the précis, a short piece that contains the major ideas or concepts of a topic. The emphasis is on an economy of words and an accurate rendering of the read or observed phenomenon. Because it is brief, word choice is critical. The ability to select the word that best represents a concept is reflective of the level of understanding of the topic. Mark Twain, a word master if ever there was one, describes word choice in this way: "The difference between the almost right word and the right word is really a large matter—it's the difference between the lightning bug and the lightning" (in Bainton, 1890). Indeed, the ability to write for accuracy and conciseness is a good indicator of the writer's knowledge of the topic and control over the form. Another Twain quote also applies: "I didn't have time to write a short letter, so I wrote a long one instead."

Peter Eagan uses summary writing in his 5th grade science classroom to check his students' understanding. Weekly labs foster inquiry-based learning of science content. At the end of each lab, students write a précis describing what they did and what was observed. One lab focused on electrical circuits involved a battery, copper wiring, a lightbulb, and a lightbulb socket, and students were asked to summarize their understanding using an explanatory text type. When Mr. Eagan read his students' summaries, he realized that several students believed that the electricity only flowed when the lightbulb was touching the wire and that the wire was "empty" when the lightbulb was removed. The following day, Mr. Eagan engaged his students in a demonstration lesson using a length of garden hose. He allowed the hose to fill with water and then covered the end so that no water could come out. He asked students to decide whether the water was still in the hose. They all agreed that the water was still in the hose. He then explained that, like the water in the hose, the electricity remained in the wires even when the lightbulb was not in the socket.

Writing-to-Learn Prompts

Writing-to-learn prompts provide students with an opportunity to clarify their thinking and allow the teacher to peek inside their heads and check for understanding. Common writing-to-learn prompts include the following:

Admit Slips: Upon entering the classroom, students write on an assigned topic. *Examples:* "Who was Gandhi and why should we care?" or "Describe the way sound waves travel."

Crystal Ball: Students describe what they think class will be about, what might happen next in the novel they're reading, or the next step in a science lab. *Example:* "How will the characters resolve their conflict?"

Awards: Students recommend someone or something for an award that the teacher has created. *Examples:* "Most helpful molecule" or "Most insidious leader."

Yesterday's News: Students summarize the information presented the day before in a video, lecture, discussion, or reading. *Example:* "Summarize our discussion of the Glorious Revolution."

Take a Stand: Students discuss their opinions about a controversial topic. *Examples:* "Is murder ever justified?" or "What's worth fighting for?"

Letters: Students write letters to others, including elected officials, family members, friends, or people who have made a difference. *Example:* Students may respond to the prompt, "Write to Oppenheimer asking him to explain his position today."

Exit Slips: As a closure activity, students write on an assigned prompt. *Example:* "The three best things I learned today are. . . ."

For example, Marisol Thayre asked her students to respond to a writing prompt in their online discussion board. Her school uses a learning management system so that students can log into their classes at any time. Ms. Thayre requires that students post in response to each question and then respond to the posts of two other students. During their discussion of *The Picture of Dorian Grey* (Wilde, 1891/1993), students were asked to respond to the following prompt:

> In a 200- to 300-word composition, defend or refute Wilde's assertion that art should be created for beauty only. Do you agree that "art for art's sake" is an acceptable motivation, or should all art have an underlying lesson, moral, or message? Use evidence from the text to support your thinking.

Discussion boards can allow students to interact with peers who are not in their same class. For example, Thomas, a student in first period, responded to a posting by Noah, a student in third period saying, "I agree with you that art should have a message. If art doesn't have a message, what's the point of spending all the time on it? I know that every drawing of mine has something behind it. I may not tell everyone what it is, but I can tell you there's always a meaning or some motivation." Ms. Thayre finds that students' written responses, both their original posts and their reaction posts, help her gauge student understanding.

RAFT

RAFT writing prompts were designed to help students take different perspectives in their writing and thus their thinking (Santa & Havens, 1995). RAFT prompts ask students to consider the following:

Role: What is the role of the writer?
Audience: To whom is the writer writing?
Format: What is the format for the writing?
Topic: What is the focus of the writing?

While RAFT prompts are typically used to teach perspective in writing, they can also be used to check for understanding. Teachers can design RAFT prompts based on all kinds of content, from lectures to videos, readings, or labs. Using RAFT prompts as a tool to check for understanding requires that the teacher know what content learning he or she expects from students and that the prompt be constructed accordingly. For example, if a 3rd grade teacher wanted to know if students understood the life cycle of insects, he or she might use the following RAFT prompt:

R: Butterfly
A: Scientist
F: Journal entry
T: My experience with complete metamorphosis

A 6th grade social studies teacher who wanted to know if students understood the life and times of Marco Polo and the importance of the Silk Road might use the following RAFT prompt:

R: Marco Polo
A: Potential recruits
F: Recruitment poster
T: Come see the Silk Road!

And finally, a geometry teacher who wanted to know if students understood the characteristics of different types of triangles might use the following RAFT prompt:

R: Scalene triangle
A: Your angles
F: Text message
T: Our unequal relationship

RAFT prompts can also be used in conjunction with texts that students read. Fifth grade teacher Paul Johnson used a number of RAFT writing prompts during his unit on slavery. Mr. Johnson knows that students need to read widely, in books that they are able to and want to read, if they are to develop strong content knowledge. He selected a number of picture books on the topic of slavery for his students to read. To check for understanding, he wrote a RAFT prompt on the inside cover of each book. Examples of the RAFT prompts from this unit are included in Figure 4.3. A sample response written by April for one of the books can be found in Figure 4.4. Note the understanding of the complex issues surrounding slavery and the personal connections this student makes with the topic under study. Upon reading this response, Mr. Johnson knew that April was developing her understanding of the history content standard as well as an appreciation for human and civil rights.

FIGURE 4.3	Sample RAFT Prompts

Minty: A Story of Young Harriet Tubman (Schroeder, 1996) **R** – Minty (Harriet Tubman) **A** – Old Ben **F** – Letter **T** – Thank you for everything you taught me	*Aunt Harriet's Underground Railroad in the Sky* (Ringgold, 1992) **R** – Cassie **A** – Bebe **F** – Invitation **T** – Let's go for a ride
Follow the Drinking Gourd (Winter, 1988) **R** – Conductor **A** – Passenger **F** – Song **T** – The path to freedom	*Sweet Clara and the Freedom Quilt* (Hopkinson, 1993) **R** – Conductor **A** – Traveler **F** – Message quilt **T** – A safe path through our town
The Underground Railroad (Stein, 1997) **R** – Dred Scott **A** – Chief Justice Roger Taney **F** – Court appeal **T** – Life as a slave in the United States	*Journey to Freedom: A Story of the Underground Railroad* (Wright, 1994) **R** – Joshua **A** – Slave catcher **F** – Response to the wanted ad **T** – My right to be free
From Slave Ship to Freedom Road (Lester, 1998) **R** – Author **A** – Reader **F** – Position statement **T** – Would you risk going to jail for someone you didn't know?	*A Picture Book of Harriet Tubman* (Adler, 1992) **R** – Slave catcher **A** – The public **F** – Wanted poster **T** – "Moses"

Tips for Success

Knowing that writing is thinking, that writing to learn clarifies students' thinking, and that writing allows teachers to check for understanding of content and ideas, wise teachers use any number of prompts to ensure their students learn. Of course, not all prompts are created equally. With some practice and experience,

FIGURE 4.4	April's RAFT Response

January 1, 1865

Dear Old Ben,

I want to thank you for being my father and teaching me about freedom. You taught me to find the North Star in the sky and follow it to the north. You showed me how to read the moss on the trees. I could know my way. I could follow the north path to freedom.

I used everything I learned from you to help other people escape on my underground railroad. I couldn't have done it without your teaching me to find the north. Thank you for everything you taught me.

Your loving daughter,
Minty

developing writing-to-learn prompts and tasks becomes easier and more fruitful. Some tips to consider as you create writing prompts to check for understanding include the following:

• The writing prompt should clearly convey the appropriate text type(s) to be utilized by specifying whether they are conveying an experience, informing or explaining, or persuading a reader.

• The writing prompt should use command words to describe the writing task, such as *analyze, compare and contrast,* or *outline.*
• The writing prompt should include format expectations, such as the length (at least 150 words), and the form or genre (a précis).
• Interweave writing-to-learn opportunities with instruction throughout a unit, not just near the end.
• Make sure that the feedback provided is aligned with the prompt itself and does not drift into other unspecified areas. Keep in mind that writing-to-learn is not process writing and therefore should not encompass every dimension of writing.

5

Using Projects and Performances to Check for Understanding

Many of us recall participating in a classroom performance or project during our school years. It may have been a school play or a science fair. Perhaps you created a diorama in a shoebox illustrating the Pilgrims' landing on Plymouth Rock. You may have constructed an animal cell out of Jell-O or built a model of a medieval castle. Whatever the project, it has undoubtedly lodged itself in your memories of school. Why are these activities so memorable? Because you were deeply invested in the outcome, you committed quite a bit of time and effort to the project or performance, and you recognized how different this was from the bulk of the assignments at which you toiled away every day.

The opportunity to apply learning to a novel situation hastens the transfer of learning. Although Bloom is well known for his work on a taxonomy of learning objectives (see Chapter 3), what is sometimes overlooked is that one of the purposes of this system was to define ways in which a transfer of learning could occur. Tasks associated with application, analysis, synthesis, and evaluation are frequently designed as projects or performances. Many of these simply could not be accomplished by filling out a worksheet or answering multiple-choice questions. Ultimately, we must witness how our students choose and use information while taking part in a meaningful activity. When we view these events as opportunities to check for understanding and not just task completion, we gain insight into the extent to which our students have transferred their learning to new situations.

In addition to using oral language, questioning techniques, and writing, effective teachers incorporate projects and performances in their classrooms to determine students' understanding of the content. In this chapter, we focus on project- and problem-based learning and the outcomes from these initiatives in terms of documenting and analyzing student learning. Barron and colleagues (1998) refer to this kind of learning as "doing with understanding" (p. 271).

Misuses of Projects and Performances in the Classroom

To use projects and performances as a tool to determine students' understanding, it is necessary to move beyond the traditional view of culminating projects. These tasks should be seen as more than just a fun or rewarding payoff for having learned all that stuff. Nancy's high school experience of representing rough endoplasmic reticulum in animal cells with uncooked lasagna noodles in Jell-O was certainly fun and memorable. Unfortunately, this fun experience did not result in her ability to recall the purpose of the endoplasmic reticulum (it synthesizes proteins). Doug's experience in making tribal masks and baskets in his 3rd grade unit of study on local Native American populations resulted in a lot of papier-mâché art, but not much understanding of the role that these items played in the daily life of the Kumeyaay. In these cases, it's likely that the "doing" part took precedence over the "understanding" part (Barron et al., 1998).

Instead, projects and performances should rightly be viewed as a part of the learning experience, and not an end point. Assigning a complex project that will only be graded once doesn't allow for students to revise and resubmit. While it is a reality that projects must invariably be finalized, too often the only time students receive any feedback is when it is too late to do anything about it. Therefore, providing interim checkpoints during multiday projects allows students to put feedback to use. Another error is in not providing students with an opportunity to reflect on their project. This is simple enough to accomplish. For example, ask students to reflect on how they are applying their feedback. Specifically, ask students to explain what has changed from the first draft to the next, and how these revisions have improved the project (Jago, 2002). These simple questions move students from compliance to active learning.

Home-school communication is essential when assigning and evaluating projects. We have seen models of California missions constructed by architect mothers and volcanoes with hydraulics installed by engineer fathers. Subsequent conversations with students reveal that they had little to do with the design or execution of the project, and as a result, they possess a limited understanding of the historical, mathematical, or scientific concepts the project was designed to foster. While we appreciate the efforts of well-meaning parents who stay up late to complete a project, it is important that they understand the intent of the assignment. After all, teachers are checking not for the parents' understanding of California history or earth science but rather their students'.

Design Principles for Projects and Performances

To maximize the potential of projects and performances to check for understanding, they must be carefully designed. Barron and colleagues (1998) describe four design principles necessary for learning to occur: "learning-appropriate goals, scaffolds for student and teacher learning, frequent opportunities for formative assessment and revision, and social organizations that promote participation" (p. 273).

Learning-Appropriate Goals

The first principle of design focuses on the overall purpose for learning. Teachers and students should understand the learning target, goal, or objective. Then the tasks, activities, or assignments can be aligned with the purpose. As we have noted elsewhere (Fisher & Frey, 2011), students need to know what they are expected to learn, and why, each day of class. When working on longer units of study, bigger questions can serve as a thread across multiple days of learning. In this case, essential questions can be used.

An essential question should cultivate a sense of curiosity and motivate students to seek answers. Essential questions should be open-ended and thought-provoking and not answerable with a simple yes or no (Wiggins & McTighe, 2013). For instance, Nancy may have better understood the functions of the organelles of an animal cell if the essential question had been "What are the common structures and functions of diverse organisms?" rather than "Can you build an animal cell using Jell-O?" Doug may have better understood the meaning of masks in Native American life if he had been furnished an essential question such as "How do humans celebrate?"

Scaffolds for Student and Teacher Learning

Most of us have learned that before engaging in a major project, it is wise to pilot a smaller version. In educational research, pilot surveys are administered to discover potential problems. Business organizations discuss "sending up a trial balloon" or "testing the waters" before launching an expensive endeavor. In similar fashion, Barron and colleagues (1998) advise providing students with a problem-based learning experience before assigning a major project. This primes students for potential difficulties and focuses their attention on the more pertinent conceptual aspects of the project. In addition, it scaffolds their understanding and provides useful feedback for the teacher, allowing misconceptions and poorly defined parameters to be addressed before too much time and effort have been invested. There are a number of scaffolds that teachers can use to support student learning as part of the projects and performances they create. As we noted in the previous chapter, questioning, prompting, and cueing are effective in providing scaffolds for students' misunderstandings. In terms of projects and performances, some tasks require specific directions or instructions. Others are designed to encourage inquiry and discovery, so instructions could be counterproductive. In some cases, a task analysis or rubric is a helpful scaffold for students. As part of the planning process, teachers should consider which content needs scaffolding. As students engage in the project or performance tasks, teachers must identify the appropriate time to scaffold and determine when the scaffold can be removed (Lajoie, 2005). In other words, students are not simply left alone to work during this time.

Frequent Opportunities for Formative Assessment and Revision

Projects and performances often demand a heavy investment of time and effort. Needless frustrations result when students have made that investment in good faith, only to discover that their end result misses the mark. More often than not, there were no systems in place to have work in progress assessed for revision. It is important to build incremental assessments into project-based assignments to prevent these difficulties. For example, Heather Anderson challenged her 10th graders to create poems in the style of Dr. Seuss (see Figure 5.1). Prior to this project, she had taught students about similes and metaphors, rhyme scheme, and word

FIGURE 5.1	The Dr. Seuss Challenge

Your poem should also have a fair share of figurative language . . . similes, metaphors, personification. Also, don't forget to control the rhythm of your poem by controlling the sounds and punctuation. Use alliteration, assonance, and onomatopoeia to make your rhythm slow down, speed up, or remain consistent.

Please hand-write your rough draft as you and your partner create it. When your rough draft is complete, use the rubric as a checklist to make sure you have all of the required elements. Once you have checked your poem with the rubric, type your final draft. Print your final draft and staple your assignment in this order: final draft (typed), rough draft (handwritten), and rubric (this paper). Make sure your heading is on the top of this page, with both partners' names on it.

_____ Consistent rhyme scheme (10)

_____ At least four stanzas with at least four lines in each stanza (20)

_____ At least one metaphor (5)

_____ At least one simile (5)

_____ At least one personification (5)

_____ Rhythm is controlled by obvious sound devices, such as alliteration, assonance, or onomatopoeia (10)

_____ Powerful verbs (5)

_____ Powerful adjectives (5)

_____ Powerful adverbs (5)

Can you write it like the man?
Can you write it with a plan?
Can you write it with a friend?
Can you write it start to end?

With your handbook as your guide,
You must think with what's inside,
Only with those words to use,
Let power word choice be your muse.

Choose your words most carefully,
From the handbook they must be,
As for thinking, take your time,
Securing in your soothing rhyme.

You CAN write it, yes, you can.
You can write it like the man.
Use your handbook and your pen.
You can do it, start to end!

choice. This project provided her students an opportunity to demonstrate their understanding of key concepts of their English class. As a side benefit, they knew that they would be visiting a local elementary school to share their poems with students. This created an authentic audience as well as additional accountability for students. Ms. Anderson provided students with the checklist found at the bottom of Figure 5.1 and met with students regularly as they drafted and revised their poems. She needed these frequent opportunities to check in with her students as they came to understand that writing like Dr. Seuss was much more difficult than it seemed. During her meetings, she took notes about areas of misunderstanding so that she could provide additional instruction before the products were completed. One of the most common errors that students made related to adverbs. They were able to rather skillfully use verbs and adjectives, but their adverb use was lacking. Noticing this early allowed Ms. Anderson to provide additional instruction so that students could revise and improve their poems.

Social Organizations That Promote Participation and a Sense of Agency

Many projects and performances involve group collaboration, and these instructional arrangements can be a source of frustration when not carefully designed and monitored. A common element in the findings about successful cooperative learning groups is that there should be both group and individual accountability (Johnson & Johnson, 1998). Therefore, it is wise to provide students with a mechanism for evaluating their own performance in the group. We have included a sample self-assessment in Figure 5.2.

Projects that are completed individually may benefit from inviting peer feedback, which can be valuable for all students. Anyone engaged in a creative endeavor knows how useful it can be to run an idea past a trusted colleague. Peer response in the classroom can offer the same advantages, but the skills required for offering and accepting feedback need to be taught. In particular, we remind our students of the following principles:

- Students determine when they need peer feedback. We don't construct an artificial schedule of when students are required to get peer feedback, only that they do so at some point during the project.

Figure **5.2**	**Self-Assessment of Group Work**

Name: _____

Date: _____

Project: _____

Members of my group:

_____

_____

_____

Please rank yourself based on your contributions to the group. Circle the number that best describes your work.

5 = Always   4 = Almost Always   3 = Sometimes   2 = Once or Twice   1 = Never

I completed my tasks on time.	5	4	3	2	1
I contributed ideas to the group.	5	4	3	2	1
I listened respectfully to the ideas of others.	5	4	3	2	1
I used other people's ideas in my work for the project.	5	4	3	2	1
When I was stuck, I sought help from my group.	5	4	3	2	1

Additional comments:

• Not everything needs peer feedback. Too much feedback can result in an overload of information.

• Teachers, not students, should offer feedback on the details and mechanics of the piece. Peer response should not turn classmates into miniature teachers. Instead, peers can provide reactions as a fellow reader, writer, or audience member related to what they understood and what might be confusing.

Problem-Based and Project-Based Learning

Both problem-based and project-based learning (PBL) can be integrated into performances. These approaches seek to replicate an authentic experience or application that occurs outside the classroom. Most experiences are designed to be collaborative, resulting in social as well as academic learning. Both problem-based and project-based learning are intended to integrate skills and content across disciplines, resulting in a holistic experience.

Although the approaches are similar, there are some differences between the two. Project-based learning is more common to elementary and secondary classrooms; problem-based learning is used less frequently (Esch, 1998). Problem-based learning is used widely in the medical field, where case studies serve as an important method for developing the skills of novices (Hmelo, 1998). Because problem-based learning is, by design, authentic to the situation, young students are more limited in their ability to successfully complete these complex assignments. Therefore, project-based learning, where a multidimensional task is defined and supported, is used more frequently in K–12 classrooms.

Projects can extend from a few days in length to weeks or even a semester, with even young children finding success. For example, project-based learning has been used in inclusive 5th and 6th grade classrooms to teach historical understanding (Ferretti, MacArthur, & Okolo, 2001). While the potential of project-based learning is appealing, Meyer, Turner, and Spencer (1997) offer cautions regarding the design of such learning experiences. Having noted that some students have less capacity for dealing with setbacks and other challenges, they state that "typical classroom goals such as accuracy, speed, and completion dates may conflict with the project-based math goals of justification, thoughtfulness, and revision" (p. 517). Keep in mind some of the design principles discussed earlier, especially access to frequent formative assessments to guide revisions. These, along with structures such as timelines and intermediate goals, can be especially helpful for students who are less persistent or who like their work to be perfect before the teacher sees it.

Performance Learning

A third type of learning opportunity used frequently in the classroom is performance, which can be presented through public or other visual means. Many performances focus on the application and synthesis of knowledge. Like project-based learning, there is an end product in mind (e.g., a poster, a blog, a musical). Not all performances are as elaborate as problem- and project-based learning assignments. Some are simpler and do not need all of the formal supports associated with PBL. For example, the creation of a graphic organizer to visually represent the influence of Muslim scholars on scientific processes, mathematics, and literature is not likely to require a series of formative assessments along the way.

The importance of performance opportunities lies in their potential for providing other outlets for students to demonstrate their mastery of concepts in ways that are not limited to more traditional school-based demonstrations such as reading, writing, and computational tasks. In many ways, performance tasks lie at the heart of differentiated instruction because they afford learners with diverse needs creative ways to show competence.

In the next section, we will discuss techniques for using performances and projects to check for understanding. All of them use principles of design discussed earlier, especially scaffolds and group interactions. Although many are public performances, some are transactions between the teacher and learner only.

Effective Techniques Using Projects and Performances

Readers' Theatre

Readers' Theatre is a classroom activity in which students read directly from scripts to tell a story or inform an audience. They do so without props, costumes, or sets. Readers' Theatre is first and foremost a *reading* activity, and students do not memorize their lines. They are, however, encouraged to use intonation, facial expression, prosody, and gestures appropriate to their characters and their characters' words. Readers' Theatre can be done with narrative or informational texts. The point is that students perform the reading.

Readers' Theatre enjoys a long history and a fairly strong research base. It has been used to improve reading fluency, vocabulary knowledge, and comprehension (Black & Stave, 2007). There are a number of ways that teachers can obtain Readers' Theatre scripts. The easiest way to find these is to type "readers' theatre scripts" into a web search engine.

Using preproduced scripts will develop students' literacy skills, especially in the areas of fluency, vocabulary knowledge, and comprehension. However, preproduced scripts are not as useful in checking for understanding (unless you're evaluating fluency). One way to use Readers' Theatre to check for understanding is to have small groups of students take a piece of text and turn it into a script. This allows the teacher to determine if the group (or individual students, for that matter) understands the main ideas of the texts. Alternatively, teachers can check students' understanding of specific content information using this method.

Sixth grade teacher Darleen Jackson uses Readers' Theatre to check for understanding of content. At one of the learning centers in her classroom, students create scripts from informational texts. The texts are selected based on the major units of study occurring at the time and represent a wide readability range. During their unit of study on ancient Egyptians, one group selected the book *Ancient Egypt* (Langley, 2005). They knew that they had to write their script, summarizing the main parts of the section they chose to read, and present the Readers' Theatre as a transition activity. Part of their performance is shown below:

Narrator: The earliest Egyptians lived in villages.

Egyptian Man 1: We decided to live in a small community.

Egyptian Man 2: It's safer when we live in a small community. Then we're not attacked by bandits or thieves.

Egyptian Man 1: We also can divide up the work. I'm a craftsman and make pottery.

Egyptian Man 2: I'm a trader who buys and sells things to keep our products moving along the Red Sea.

Egyptian Woman 1: There's no mention of what I'm doing for work, probably just taking care of the house and babies.

Narrator: Each small community developed their own leaders and religions.

When she listened to the group's Readers' Theatre presentation, Ms. Jackson knew that her students were developing an understanding of life in ancient Egypt. She was pleased that they questioned the role of women in ancient Egypt, but wanted to be sure that they understood the development of commerce in this society. She planned to subsequently meet with this group in guided instruction and have them summarize their understandings to date.

Multimedia Presentations

Multimedia presentations provide learners an opportunity to share what they know as they combine text, graphics, video, sound, and even animation. Although such projects were unthinkable just a few years ago due to the costs of hardware and software involved, students today can produce complex products. The digital revolution has provided students with new ways of demonstrating their knowledge and has given teachers new ways of checking for understanding.

Fourth grade teacher Michael Kluth spends much of the school year focused on the human body and its systems. Throughout the year, students develop and present several PowerPoint presentations. Mr. Kluth's students have to read widely about the body systems they've selected in order to develop their understanding of the systems and to create their presentations. Mr. Kluth knows that these multimedia presentations allow him to check his students' understanding of the human body. He also knows that the projects enable his students to practice their listening and speaking skills. Groups present a body system each month and listen to at least 10 other presentations during that time (some of his students are in the library conducting their research while others are presenting). During these listening opportunities, students take notes. This continual review of body systems and the cumulative knowledge students gain from developing their own multimedia presentations, as well as from listening to and taking notes on the presentations of others, allow Mr. Kluth the opportunity to evaluate his students in a meaningful way. As Mr. Kluth says, "The first set of presentations is just okay. They learn more for each system they complete and incorporate what they've learned from others. I can listen to the presentation and provide feedback on the content, common misconceptions, and their developing language skills. I also support them in creating more dynamic presentations with animation, video, and sound."

Students in Heather Anderson's 10th grade English class were invited to use Facebook to demonstrate their understanding of the essential question: What's worth fighting, or even dying, for? They had read a number of books over the course of the year about "worthy causes" and had engaged in an interdisciplinary unit on the Holocaust. Toward the end of the year, Ms. Anderson wanted to know if her students had identified a cause that was very important to them and if they could explain that cause to others. She created two projects for her students: a

Facebook page and a brochure (see Figure 5.3). Students' interests were varied, ranging from pages on Islamaphobia to saving polar bears to providing information about a rare disability called CHARGE syndrome. As students constructed their pages, Ms. Anderson could log onto Facebook and check on their progress as well as the accuracy of their work.

Electronic and Paper Portfolios

A portfolio is a collection of items intended to reflect a body of work. Architects and artists assemble professional portfolios to show clients their best work and to demonstrate their range of expertise. Educational portfolios differ slightly from those used by professionals in that they are designed to reflect a student's process of learning (Tierney, 1998). They are not meant to serve as a scrapbook of random ephemera gathered during the school year. At their best, they can provide another way to check for understanding. However, this requires that the student choose the evidence that best illustrates his or her cognitive processes. An added benefit of portfolios is that they can involve parents in the process of checking their child's understanding.

A challenge of portfolio creation is making decisions about what should be used. Wilcox (1997) proposes a model for portfolios that emphasizes the cognitive processes of learning, suggesting that the following items be included:

- Reading artifacts that make connections through reading, such as diagrams, outlines, and summaries.
- Thinking artifacts that construct our knowledge base, such as mind maps, steps to problem solving, and responses to prompts.
- Writing artifacts that make meaning through writing, such as self-evaluations, a publication piece, and reflections on a learning experience.
- Interacting artifacts that share and scaffold ideas, such as peer assessments, brainstorming charts, and a problem and solution.
- Demonstrating artifacts that show application and transfer of new learning, such as a project or exhibition. (p. 35)

Portfolios can be electronic or in a traditional paper-based format, usually stored in three-ring binders. Paper portfolios are generally easier for younger children to handle, as they can easily add new items and remove others with little

Figure 5.3	A Worthy Cause Project

We are often presented with issues that impact our community, state, nation, and world. Are you passionate about recycling? Do you wish there was a cure for cancer or AIDS? Have you ever thought about an animal becoming extinct and what you could do to help? When you stop and **THINK,** there are endless causes in our world for you to support and become an activist for.

You will create a **Facebook** page and **pamphlet** that *educates* your peers at HSHMC about a cause you are passionate about. Select a cause that you feel is worthy of your time. This competency is worth **100 points.** The points are broken down below.

Facebook page portion: (total of 50 points)		
Create a Facebook page with links, updates, descriptions	(20 pts.)	
Minimum of 2 status posts per week, 3 must be links, one must be video	(15 pts.)	
Minimum of 40 LIKES	(15 pts.)	

Pamphlet portion: (total of 50 points)		
Cover has the title, image, and your name	(5 pts.)	
Description of your cause (min. 5 sentences)	(10 pts.)	
List 3–5 important facts	(5 pts.)	
Map of where this is occurring	(5 pts.)	
Demographics of who/what is impacted	(5 pts.)	
Minimum of 3 images in your brochure	(5 pts.)	
Contact information (websites, telephone numbers)	(5 pts.)	
Upcoming events (celebrations, day, movie, anniversary date, races, etc.)	(5 pts.)	
Pamphlet is attractive and well organized	(5 pts.)	
Correct spelling and grammar	(must be edited)	

Date Checklist		
Cause selected and approved by teacher and parents	Monday 5/9	
Facebook page started	Friday 5/13	
Rough draft of pamphlet	Friday 5/20	
Final due date for Facebook and pamphlet	Friday 5/27	

assistance from an adult. Digital portfolios are often used with older students, especially because this format has become essential to 21st century classrooms. Experiences with the design and assembly of digital presentations also prepare students to create the electronic portfolios expected in higher education and the workplace.

Navigating the creation and maintenance of portfolios, whether paper or digital, with students can be tricky. On the one hand, students need guidance in developing portfolios; on the other, the question of ownership in such a personal expression can be negatively affected by the required nature of many such assignments. The balance lies in teaching about types of artifacts, as suggested by Wilcox, and resisting formulaic approaches that require students to furnish three examples of this and four examples of that. The danger of such prescriptive portfolio assignments is that portfolios are reduced to filling in the blanks, thus reducing checking for understanding to task completion only.

Eighth grade teacher Tahira Birhanu taught her English class the basics of electronic portfolios at the beginning of the year so that students could choose to create them as a method for demonstrating their understanding of the works read and discussed in class. Her students know that a title card, table of contents, and buttons to activate links to sections of the portfolio are a must. Her primary interest is in analyzing the reflective and elaborative pieces the students include explaining the reading, writing, thinking, interacting, and demonstrating artifacts selected for the portfolio. One of the students in her class, Madison, chose to construct an electronic portfolio to explain her work with her literature circle, which had read *Project Mulberry* (Park, 2005). The story of a Korean American girl who rebels against being stereotyped as obedient and studious resonated with Madison, and she was eager to write about her thoughts. She included a collage comprising images captured from the Internet that represented the conflict the protagonist experienced. Madison also located links to websites that explained how silkworms are raised, since they become the focus of the science project discussed in the book. In addition to the collage and information, Madison included examples of notes she took during her reading and samples from the journal she kept for her literature circle group.

One of the reflective pieces that Madison wrote about regarding taking notes was included in her portfolio:

When I heard we had to write notes as we read, all I could think of was, "Busy work!" I'm a good reader, and I don't need to be assigned reading to get into a good book. Taking notes was just going to slow me down. But when I reread some of my notes from earlier in the book, I could see how much my thinking had changed. I noticed that at the beginning of the book I thought that Julia was right to dislike anything that was "too Korean. " My mom's always making me listen to all these old stories about people I hardly know. But when I read my notes for this project I started thinking about how maybe I wasn't being fair to my mom, just like Julia wasn't being fair to hers.

Ms. Birhanu was pleased to see how Madison had turned a reading artifact (her notes) into a demonstration of her transfer of learning.

Visual Displays of Information

Visual displays of information require students to represent knowledge in a nonlinguistic fashion, typically using images or movement to do so. There is evidence that students who generate visual representations of a concept are better able to understand and recall the concept (Ritchie & Karge, 1996). Edens and Potter (2003) studied 184 4th and 5th graders who were learning about the law of conservation of energy. Those randomly assigned students who generated drawings scored higher on a test of conceptual knowledge and possessed fewer misconceptions than their peers who wrote in a science journal. They also noted in their study that the drawings themselves served as another means for assessing misconceptions and inaccuracies. It is likely that the use of visual representations of understanding assist the learner in building mental models (Mayer & Gallini, 1990). We discuss four types of visual representations below.

Graphic organizers. These are one of the most common and well-researched tools used in reading comprehension (Moore & Readence, 1984). While the instructional implications for graphic organizers are clear, the role that these visual representations play in assessment is less so. When teachers are checking for understanding, it seems reasonable to suggest that asking students to create a visual representation of their knowledge would be valuable. We're not suggesting that teachers learn to assess or evaluate the graphic organizers (e.g., how well the web is drawn) but rather that we use the construction of graphic organizers as a source of information to determine what students know and do not know.

As we have learned from the evidence on thinking maps (see, e.g., www.thinkingmaps.com), students need to be taught to use a variety of visual tools and graphic organizers. We believe that this is necessary regardless of whether graphic organizers are used for instruction or to check for understanding. Simply photocopying a graphic organizer and requiring that students fill it out will not ensure deep learning or provide an authentic assessment opportunity. Figure 5.4 contains a list of various types of graphic organizers and thinking maps with which students should be familiar.

Physics teacher Jesse Nunez uses graphic organizers in his class to check students' understanding of content. He teaches his students a number of tools early in the school year and then invites them to use different tools to demonstrate their content knowledge. He does not provide photocopies of graphic organizers or require that students all use the same graphic organizer at the same time. During their unit of study on states of matter, Arian created a concept map explaining her knowledge of solids, liquids, and gases (see Figure 5.5). Mr. Nunez reviewed Arian's concept map and noted that she understood each of the three states of matter but wondered if she comprehended the interactions and relationships between and among these states of matter.

Inspiration. Like many things in our world, graphic organizers can also go digital. The Inspiration and Kidspiration software programs allow users to create visual tools—graphic organizers—on the screen (see www.inspiration.com for information). Current versions of the software allow users to import text, transform ideas and graphics, and select from a range of graphic organizers and tools.

Royer and Royer (2004) wondered if there was any difference in the complexity of the concept maps students would create if they had access to computers to complete the tasks. They compared the graphic organizers created by 52 students in biology classes that used either paper and pencil or computers with Inspiration software. Their findings suggest that there are significant positive outcomes when students create graphic organizers in a digital environment. Mastropieri, Scruggs, and Graetz (2003) document similar results and make similar recommendations for students who struggle with reading or who have disabilities.

Figure 5.4	Graphic Organizers and Definitions

primitives	Thinking Maps and the Frame	expanded maps
	The Circle Map is used for seeking context. This tool enables students to generate relevant information about a topic as represented in the center of the circle. This map is often used for brainstorming.	
	The Bubble Map is designed for the process of describing attributes. This map is used to identify character traits (language arts), cultural traits (social studies), properties (sciences), or attributes (mathematics).	
	The Double Bubble Map is used for comparing and contrasting two things, such as characters in a story, historical figures, or social systems. It is also used for prioritizing which information is most important within a comparison.	
	The Tree Map enables students to do both inductive and deductive classification. Students learn to create general concepts, (main) ideas, or category headings at the top of the tree, and supporting ideas and specific details in the branches below.	
	The Brace Map is used for identifying the part–whole, physical relationships of an object. By representing whole–part and part–subpart relationships, this map supports students' spatial reasoning and understanding of how to determine physical boundaries.	
	The Flow Map is based on the use of flowcharts. It is used by students for showing sequences, order, timelines, cycles, actions, steps, and directions. This map also focuses students on seeing the relationships between stages and substages of events.	
	The Multi-Flow Map is a tool for seeking causes of events and the effects. The map expands when showing historical causes and for predicting future events and outcomes. In its most complex form, it expands to show the interrelationships of feedback effects in a dynamic system.	
	The Bridge Map provides a visual pathway for creating and interpreting analogies. Beyond the use of this map for solving analogies on standardized tests, this map is used for developing analogical reasoning and metaphorical concepts for deeper content learning.	

The Frame

The "metacognitive" Frame is not one of the eight Thinking Maps. It may be drawn around any of the maps at any time as a "meta-tool" for identifying and sharing one's frame of reference for the information found within one of the Thinking Maps. These frames include personal histories, culture, belief systems, and influences such as peer groups and the media.

Reprinted with permission. Thinking Maps® is a registered trademark of Thinking Maps, Inc. For use of Thinking Maps® in the classroom, please visit www.thinkingmaps.com.

Figure
5.5

Arian's Concept Map

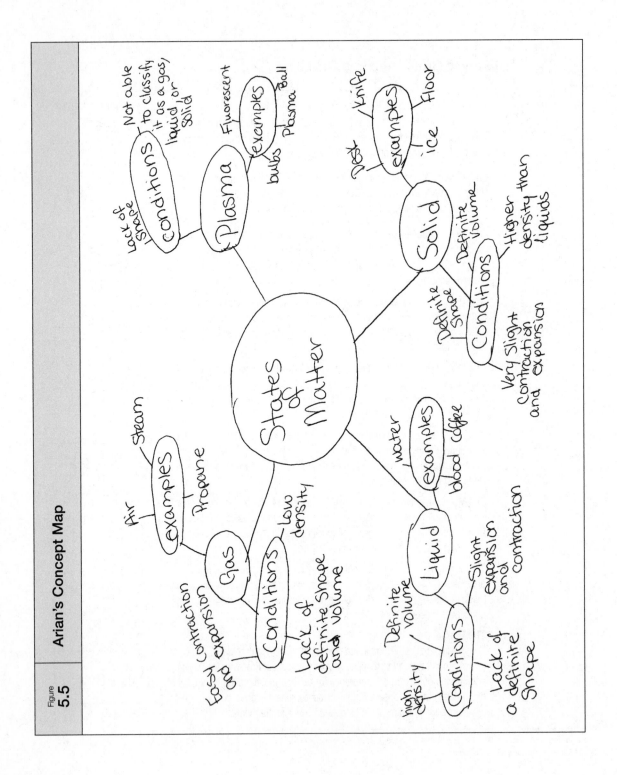

During their study of insects, complete and incomplete metamorphosis, and life cycles, the students in Jenny Olson's class spent time at a learning center creating visual representations of their understanding using Inspiration. Javier created the visual representation—a concept map—of complete metamorphosis found in Figure 5.6. Ms. Olson noticed that Javier had an understanding of the stages of complete metamorphosis and had collected some interesting details about each stage from the various books he had read. However, she also noted that his visual representation did not communicate the stage and cycle information critical to understanding the process of metamorphosis and the insect life cycle. She decided to meet with him and discuss his graphic organizer. Through questioning, she led Javier to understand how to represent his learning visually. She also had the opportunity to solidify his understanding that eggs become larvae, larvae become pupae, pupae become adults, and then the adults lay eggs.

Foldables. Foldables are three-dimensional interactive graphic organizers developed by Zike (1992). They provide students with a way of manipulating concepts and information in ways that are far more kinesthetic than ordinary worksheets. Paper is folded into simple shapes that reflect the conceptual relationships represented by the notes. Sixth grade social studies teacher Tim Valdes asked students to compare and contrast the Athenians and Spartans of ancient Greece. His students had been working with interactive graphic organizers since the beginning of the school year, so they were able to select their own way of representing this information. Arturo chose to make a three-tab book with a Venn diagram drawn on the front. Under each flap, he wrote information about both city-states. Arturo's choice of an organizer and the information he included gave Mr. Valdes insight into the knowledge his student possessed, as well as the mental model he used. Arturo's Foldable is represented in Figure 5.7.

Dioramas. Though some believe dioramas are old-fashioned, we are proponents of dioramas as a method of performance. Unlike the dioramas of our youth, which tended to emphasize the composition of the final product over the learning invested in its development, the potential of a diorama is akin to any other visual representation of knowledge. Dioramas are miniature models of a scene from the physical, social, biological, or narrative world, traditionally built inside a shoebox turned on its side.

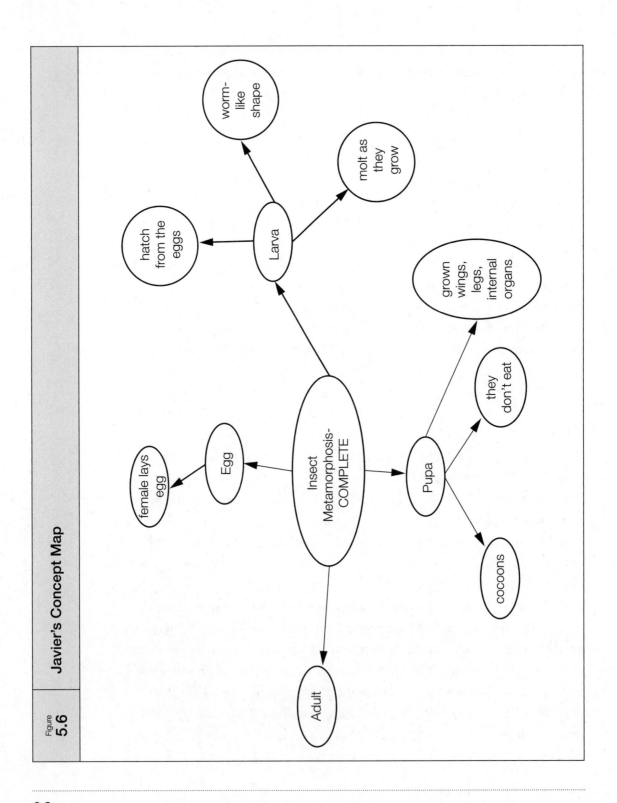

Figure 5.6 Javier's Concept Map

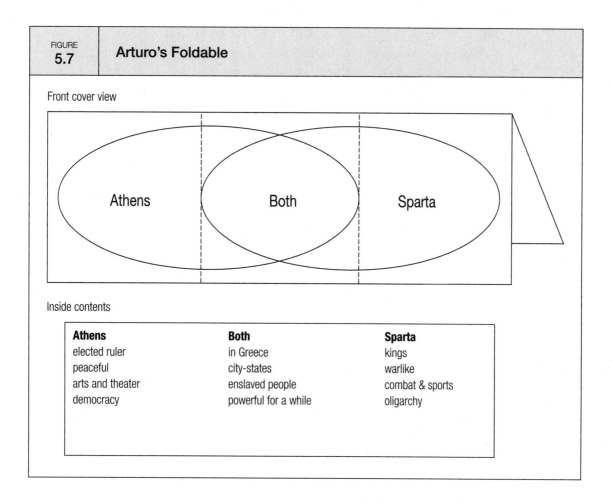

FIGURE
5.7

Arturo's Foldable

Front cover view

Athens | Both | Sparta

Inside contents

Athens
elected ruler
peaceful
arts and theater
democracy

Both
in Greece
city-states
enslaved people
powerful for a while

Sparta
kings
warlike
combat & sports
oligarchy

Louis Daguerre, the inventor of the daguerreotype, was the first to conceive the use of dioramas. He was a set designer by trade, and he developed large-scale dioramas (more than 20 feet in length) for public display, their subject usually an architectural wonder (Maggi, 1999). Using a *chiaroscuro* painting technique (the arrangement or treatment of light and dark parts in a pictorial work of art) and lighting methods learned in the theater, Daguerre introduced the world to a unique style of visual storytelling.

It is this visual narrative that offers a way of checking for understanding. By examining the information represented in the diorama, as well as talking with students about how they represented the information, you can check for their understanding of the concepts. Third grade teacher Belinda Mullins uses dioramas as a way for students to demonstrate what they have learned about animals they have researched in science. Emily chose to learn about the Mexican free-tailed bat. She constructed a diorama that included a drawing of a small brown bat flying out of a cave. Emily hung the bat drawing from a piece of yarn attached to the top of the diorama to represent flight, and she lined the inside of the box with black construction paper. She glued small "googly eyes" purchased from a craft store at the opening of the cave. Tiny drops of brown puff paint dotted the inside of the display. She explained to Ms. Mullins that this bat lives in caves and flies at night. Some caves are filled with millions of Mexican free-tailed bats, making them some of the largest colonies on Earth (that's what the "googly eyes" were for). Ms. Mullins told Emily that she understood that the black construction paper represented the night sky, but what were the brown dots of paint meant to be? Emily replied, "Those are the mosquitoes they eat every night!" By making sure that she met with Emily and each of her students, Ms. Mullins was able to check their understanding about the animals they had selected as the subject for their first science research project.

Public Performances

The act of performing publicly can be a memorable experience for students and teachers. As noted earlier in this chapter, public performances can also be used as a means for checking for understanding. Podlozny's (2000) meta-analysis indicates that when students received instruction on public performance, there was an increase in comprehension and, to a lesser extent, reading achievement. In recent years, many high schools have begun to require public exhibitions of knowledge as part of the graduation requirements for seniors.

Rita Elwardi and Sheri Sevenbergen's students in their high school ESL classes engage in an extended public performance of their learning in an exhibition that has come to be known as "The Quilt Celebration. " Their students come from every continent except Antarctica and Australia, and together they represent the range of human experiences associated with immigration to America. Over the course of the year, students construct a quilt made of individual squares that visually represent their stories. They write poetry collaboratively for public performance at the celebration. Students discuss their transformation through learning and their plans to continue their education. The celebration is attended by a large audience of families, faculty, students, and community members. As you can imagine, the event is moving; audience members are sometimes brought to tears as they listen to the insightful comments of these adolescents. However, Ms. Elwardi and Ms. Sevenbergen also use these public performances as a way to check for understanding. As Ms. Elwardi notes, "They need to be able to tell their own stories, and to relate who they are and what they stand for to others. As new arrivals to this country, it's easy for them to become intimidated by the language. This event gives them an opportunity to tell their story more formally, which is practice for a lifetime of effective communication. " The students wrote and performed several poems for the Quilt Celebration in 2006, one of which can be found in Figure 5.8.

FIGURE 5.8	Poem from the Quilt Celebration

I used to be a grain of sand,
caught in an oyster shell,
but now I am a pearl,
reflecting the luminous moon
of possible dreams.

I used to be a closed fist,
clenched in anger,
but now I am an open hand,
extending friendship.

I used to be a caterpillar,
always stuck on a leaf,
but now I am a butterfly—
flying for freedom and looking for love.

I used to be the starless night,
hiding my dreams in darkness,
but now I am a prism of light
illuminating my way into the future.

I used to be a hard lump of coal
under the ground,
but now I am a glittering diamond,
valuable and precious.

I used to be a blank piece of paper,
but now I am a journal full of ideas.

I used to be a moon,
sometimes full, sometimes half,
sometimes just a sliver of myself,
but now I am a star sending light
to unknown worlds.

I used to be a paper crane,
folded to resemble something real,
but now my wings take me
to the height of my hopes and dreams.

I used to be lead, held by a pencil,
but now I am the words,
bringing ideas to life on paper.

I used to be a seed,
fallen to the ground,
but now I am a giant tree
with branches that give others shade.

Tips for Success

Projects and performances are an underused but critical method of checking for understanding. These displays offer students an opportunity to use new learning to create original works, allowing a transfer of learning to occur. By using the design principles put forth by Barron and colleagues (1998), teachers can ensure that more meaningful work is generated. While some tasks require extensive preparation for their execution, such as portfolios and public performances, many others, such as visual displays of information and Readers' Theatre, are easily integrated into daily classroom practice.

Some tips to consider as you consider the use of projects and performances to check for understanding include the following:

• Plan the project and performance in advance and clearly link it to learning goals. Students, rightfully so, want to know why they're doing specific tasks, not just how to do them.

• Before the project or performance is introduced to students, make sure that you have all of the necessary supplies. Students work at different paces and will need supplies at different times.

• Consistent with the appropriate uses of rubrics and checklists, review the criteria for success with students in advance of them completing tasks. Students should have an understanding of the expectations before they are provided feedback. Ideally, students will co-construct the rubric with the teacher, which facilitates understanding of the task and encourages engagement with the learning goals.

• Plan for sufficient time for students to complete the project or performance. These types of learning tasks tend to take longer than expected. Cutting students off when their work is not yet complete sends the message that their understanding is not that important after all. Ending projects prematurely also prevents the teacher from developing an understanding of students' instructional needs.

6

Using Tests to Check for Understanding

In this era of accountability, student understanding is ultimately measured by tests. In this chapter, we explore the use of tests to determine what students know and don't know. We discuss the schools that are beating the odds by providing students with test format practice throughout the year and teaching students about tests as a genre (similar to biographies or science fiction). We also provide guidelines for creating a variety of constructed-response test items, including multiple choice, short answer, dichotomous choices, and essays.

We recognize the anxiety that tests can provoke in students. This anxiety is heightened for those who feel unprepared, unskilled, or psychologically uneasy. We have both witnessed our share of students who have become emotionally distraught and even physically ill at the sight of a test. Empathy for our students should be balanced with hard questions about our role in their apprehension. If tests are really intended to check for understanding, we need our students to perform at their optimal level. What factors are contributing to their mental state? Have we adequately prepared them for the content being tested? Have we taught them to be "test-wise"? Can we recognize the difference in student performance results when either factor is problematic?

We believe that information is power and when teachers understand the purposes and limitations of various tests and approaches, their students will profit.

However, our students cannot fully benefit if we do not take the time to explain how tests work. Even more important, we need to help our students understand the purposes for testing. Far too many students believe that their futures ride on the outcome of a single test. Sadly, that is sometimes true. We are appalled at reports of informal reading inventories being misused to make in-grade retention decisions for 1st graders. We worry about high school students who decide to drop out of school because their performance on the state exit exam has confirmed in their minds that they are not smart enough to succeed academically. And we are depressed when a student raises his or her hand in the middle of an engaging lesson to ask, "Is this going to be on the test?"

While we cannot single-handedly change the testing climate overnight, we can create classrooms where testing is understood and appreciated by teachers and students for what it can accomplish. There are two implications for this proposal. The first is that we must understand what different tests do and share that information with our students. The second is that we must develop a classroom climate that empowers students in their quest to check their own understanding. In other words, testing should not have the sole purpose of extracting a grade. It can be a method for learners to monitor their own understanding and to act upon their own learning. When students are encouraged to set goals, and tests are linked to those goals, learners can be motivated to actively engage in their own learning (Tuckman, 1998). Keep in mind, too, that if you are checking for understanding in the many ways discussed in this book, the need for a single test to evaluate student performance is eliminated. Furthermore, students of teachers who are continually checking for understanding benefit from assessment and feedback across their learning day.

Why Use Tests?

Tests and assessments are used for a variety of purposes. Lapp, Fisher, Flood, and Cabello (2001) identify the following four reasons tests and assessments are commonly used:

• Diagnosing individual student needs (e.g., assessing developmental status, monitoring and communicating student progress, certifying competency, determining needs);

- Informing instruction (e.g., evaluating instruction, modifying instructional strategies, identifying instructional needs);
- Evaluating programs; or
- Providing accountability information. (p. 7)

Given these diverse uses of tests and assessments, it seems reasonable to suggest that there are, or have been, misuses of this technique. As a principal friend of ours says, "You can't fatten the cattle just by weighing 'em." We agree. You have to *do* something with the information you get from tests and assessments. It's important to remember that there are good and appropriate uses of tests. In checking for understanding, tests are used for the second purpose noted above—to inform instruction. Before we continue with our discussion on the appropriate uses of tests and assessments, let's consider their potential misuses.

Misuses of Tests in the Classroom

Consider the history of educational testing. Tests of one kind or another have been around for a long time (Webb, 2006). But the world changed with the advent of the IQ test (Gould, 1981). The IQ test brought science, the scientific process, and "hard data" to education. At this point in history, most fields and professions were being influenced by the successes in manufacturing, Progressive Era thinking in general, and the focus on the efficiency movement in particular (Gould, 2001). In essence, the dominant idea of the time was that the scientific study of a problem would lead to answers and an unambiguous solution. Professionals, such as physicians, looked for specific tools they could use in studying and solving issues.

The IQ test appeared to be the scientific tool that would work for education. It allowed educators to function as professionals or experts with a set of tools at their disposal. Educators could "scientifically" evaluate a child's ability—their intelligence quotient, as Terman (1916) labeled it. Using the IQ test, educators believed that they could determine the future success of a child and track the child into appropriately demanding classes based on his or her ability. To educators of the day living in the Progressive Era, this seemed both scientific and child focused; it wouldn't burden the "mentally deficient" (in the vocabulary of the time), nor would it prevent gifted and talented students from accessing more challenging work.

Over the next several decades, educators debated the usefulness of the IQ test and searched for more valid, reliable, and culturally sensitive measures of children's intellectual ability. In the 1960s and 1970s, IQ tests began to fall out of favor, partially because of racially and culturally specific test questions and partially because they did not deliver on their promise. In 1964, the New York City Board of Education eliminated IQ testing entirely. In 1983, Howard Gardner argued that reason, intelligence, logic, and knowledge are not synonymous; introduced the world to a theory of multiple intelligences; and reaffirmed Binet's belief that intelligence was complex and could not be easily measured by a single score.

The current focus on testing is the latest cycle of the on-again, off-again use of tests in public schooling. And it should come as no surprise that there are critics (and concerned individuals) of this high-accountability phase of education (see, e.g., Kohn, 2000; Popham, 2003). Critics typically cluster their concerns about standardized testing into the following four areas (Yeh, 2005):

- Narrowing the curriculum by excluding subject matter not tested. For example, with a significant focus on reading and math, the concern is that social studies, music, and art are being neglected because they are not commonly tested.
- Excluding topics either not tested or not likely to appear on the test even within tested subjects. For example, oral language (i.e., speaking and listening) is not commonly tested as part of the language arts and is therefore at risk in the classroom.
- Reducing learning to the memorization of easily recalled facts for multiple-choice testing. For example, students are taught to memorize math formulas rather than understand how and when to use such formulas.
- Devoting too much classroom time to test preparation rather than learning. For example, spending the first 10 minutes of each period focused on sample test questions rather than the content students need to know in order to master the subject or discipline.

More recently, the increased use of online testing platforms has raised new concerns about the preparedness of schools and districts to deal with network, hardware, and connectivity issues. In addition, educators are concerned that some students are not prepared to take online tests. Many of these pertain to the technology demands. The results of the spring 2013 scientific pilot administered by the Smarter Balanced Assessment Consortium revealed four challenges faced by students (Phelan, 2013, ¶5):

- Moving between two or more screens
- Operating spreadsheets and calculators
- Manipulating virtual objects such as geometric constructions
- Editing electronic text

In response to these findings, the Fresno (CA) County Office of Education has developed a useful plan for developing the needed technology skills of students. These include making sure that K–2 students learn the icons used for basic operations, such as the trash feature. Students in grades 3–5 should be learning how to cut and paste text and images in digital documents. Middle school students should have experience at creating simple databases, while high school students should become adept at creating and utilizing spreadsheets. A complete version of this plan can be found at http://commoncore.fcoe.org/sites/commoncore.fcoe.org/files/resources/FCOE_TechSkills_Flowchart_2012.pdf.

Interestingly, in her study comparing higher- and lower-performing schools, Langer (2001) found that teachers in the higher-performing schools use tests as an opportunity to "revise and reformulate their curriculum" (p. 860). She reports, "While they do practice format before a test, not much teaching time is devoted to it. Rather, infusion is the key" (p. 861). Langer finds a direct contrast in lower-performing schools. There, teachers "treated tests as an additional hurdle, separated from their literacy curriculum. In these schools the test-taking focus seems to be on teaching to the test-taking skills rather than gaining skills and knowledge" (p. 862). This application of testing is not the only thing that teachers in higher-performing schools do differently; they also infuse literacy skills into and across the curriculum.

This is similar to the work done by Fullan, Hill, and Crévola (2006), who note that an educational "breakthrough" is possible. In their words:

The key to this transformation lies in the smart use of data to drive instruction. Currently, many school systems collect data and feed it back to districts and schools. Much of this feedback is rudimentary and surface level. Where deeper feedback occurs, teachers are not helped to know what to do with it. Even if the data are better analyzed, teachers do not know how to translate the information into powerful, focused instruction that responds to individual students' needs. (p. xvi)

We agree with Fullan and his colleagues and the findings from the Langer study. In our experience, it is through checking for understanding that students learn to demonstrate their knowledge in a variety of ways (including on tests) and that teachers can make needed curricular changes and implement instructional innovations. While we are focused on checking for understanding using formative rather than summative assessments (such as standardized state tests), we do know that regular practice, feedback, and focused instruction based on individual student needs will change learning outcomes (Fisher, Lapp, & Flood, 2005). Let's consider a number of ways to design tests that can provide teachers with opportunities to check for understanding.

Using Tests to Check for Understanding

Checking for understanding using tests is dependent in part on the design and development of good test items. Figure 6.1 provides a checklist useful in the development of different types of testing items. However, checking for understanding using tests is equally dependent on the analysis of student responses. Of course, this is not unique to tests. All of the systems for checking for understanding we have discussed in this book require an analysis of student responses as well as instructional decisions based on those individual responses.

Multiple Choice

Multiple-choice items are probably the most common type of objective test question (Linn & Miller, 2005). They provide the teacher with an opportunity to gauge students' understanding in a fairly quick and efficient manner. They also are easy to analyze in that incorrect responses can be clustered as percentages and teachers can easily determine which of the incorrect responses students most commonly selected. A list of the advantages and disadvantages of multiple-choice items can be found in Figure 6.2.

Multiple-choice items consist of two parts: a stem and a number of response options. In other words, the multiple-choice item presents a problem and a list of possible solutions. Both of these parts are important to the creation of a good test item.

Figure 6.1	Checklist for Creating Assessments

All Items
- ☐ Is this the most appropriate type of item to use for the intended learning outcomes?
- ☐ Does each item or task require students to demonstrate the performance described in the specific learning outcome it measures (relevance)?
- ☐ Does each item present a clear and definite task to be performed (clarity)?
- ☐ Is each item or task presented in simple, readable language and free from excessive verbiage (conciseness)?
- ☐ Does each item provide an appropriate challenge (ideal difficulty)?
- ☐ Does each item have an answer that would be agreed upon by experts (correctness)?
- ☐ Is there a clear basis for awarding partial credit on items or tasks with multiple points (scoring rubric)?
- ☐ Is each item or task free from technical errors and irrelevant clues (technical soundness)?
- ☐ Is each test item free from cultural bias?
- ☐ Have the items been set aside for a time before reviewing them (or having them reviewed by a colleague)?

Short-Answer Items
- ☐ Can the items be answered with a number, symbol, word, or brief phrase?
- ☐ Has textbook language been avoided?
- ☐ Have the items been stated so that only one response is correct?
- ☐ Are the answer blanks equal in length (for fill-in responses)?
- ☐ Are the answer blanks (preferably one per item) at the end of the items, preferably after a question?
- ☐ Are the items free of clues (such as *a* or *an*)?
- ☐ Has the degree of precision been indicated for numerical answers?
- ☐ Have the units been indicated when numerical answers are expressed in units?

Binary (True–False) and Multiple-Binary Items
- ☐ Can each statement be clearly judged true or false with only one concept per statement?
- ☐ Have specific determiners (e.g., usually, always) been avoided?
- ☐ Have trivial statements been avoided?
- ☐ Have negative statements (especially double negatives) been avoided?
- ☐ Does a superficial analysis suggest a wrong answer?
- ☐ Are opinion statements attributed to some source?
- ☐ Are the true and false items approximately equal in length?
- ☐ Is there approximately an equal number of true and false items?
- ☐ Has a detectable pattern of answers (e.g., T, F, T, F) been avoided?

Matching Items
- ☐ Is the material for the two lists homogeneous?
- ☐ Is the list of responses longer or shorter than the list of premises?
- ☐ Are the responses brief and on the right-hand side?
- ☐ Have the responses been placed in alphabetical or numerical order?
- ☐ Do the directions indicate the basis for matching?
- ☐ Do the directions indicate how many times each response may be used?
- ☐ Are all of the matching items on the same page?

(continued)

Figure 6.1	**Checklist for Creating Assessments** (*continued*)

Multiple-Choice Items

☐ Does each item stem present a meaningful problem?
☐ Is there too much information in the stem?
☐ Are the item stems free of irrelevant material?
☐ Are the item stems stated in positive terms (if possible)?
☐ If used, has negative wording been given special emphasis (e.g., capitalized)?
☐ Are the distractors brief and free of unnecessary words?
☐ Are the distractors similar in length and form to the answer?
☐ Is there only one correct or clearly best answer?
☐ Are the distractors based on specific misconceptions?
☐ Are the items free of clues that point to the answer?
☐ Are the distractors and answer presented in sensible (e.g., alphabetical, numerical) order?
☐ Has "all of the above" been avoided and has "none of the above" been used judiciously?
☐ If a stimulus is used, is it necessary for answering the item?
☐ If a stimulus is used, does it require use of skills sought to be assessed?

Essay Items

☐ Are the questions designed to measure higher-level learning outcomes?
☐ Does each question clearly indicate the response expected (including extensiveness)?
☐ Are students aware of the basis on which their answers will be evaluated?
☐ Are appropriate time limits provided for responding to the questions?
☐ Are students aware of the time limits and/or point values for each question?
☐ Are all students required to respond to the same questions?

Performance Items

☐ Does the item focus on learning outcomes that require complex cognitive skills and student performances?
☐ Does the task represent both the content and skills that are central to learning outcomes?
☐ Does the item minimize dependence on skills that are irrelevant to the intended purpose of the assessment task?
☐ Does the task provide the necessary scaffolding for students to be able to understand the task and achieve the task?
☐ Do the directions clearly describe the task?
☐ Are students aware of the basis (expectations) on which their performances will be evaluated in terms of scoring rubrics?

For the Assessment as a Whole

☐ Are the items of the same type grouped together on the test (or within sections, sets)?
☐ Are the items arranged from easy to more difficult within sections or the test as a whole?
☐ Are items numbered in sequence, indicating so if the test continues on subsequent pages?
☐ Are all answer spaces clearly indicated and is each answer space related to its corresponding item?
☐ Are the correct answers distributed in such a way that there is no detectable pattern?
☐ Is the test material well-spaced, legible, and free of typos?
☐ Are there directions for each section of the test and the test as a whole?
☐ Are the directions clear and concise?

Adapted from *Measurement and assessment in teaching* (9th ed.), by R. L. Linn and M. D. Miller, 2005, Upper Saddle River, NJ: Merrill Prentice Hall.

Figure 6.2	Advantages and Disadvantages of Multiple-Choice Items	
Advantages		**Disadvantages**
Allows for assessment of a wide range of learning objectives, from factual to evaluative understanding		Quality items are difficult and time-consuming to develop
Analyzing patterns of incorrect responses may provide diagnostic information		Tendency for items to focus on low-level learning objectives
Permits wide sampling and broad coverage of content domain due to students' ability to respond to many items		Assessment results may be biased by students' reading ability and test savvy
Allows the comparison and evaluation of related ideas, concepts, or theories		May overestimate learning due to the ability to utilize an elimination process for answer selection
Permits manipulation of difficulty level by adjusting the degree of similarity among response options		Does not measure the ability to organize and express ideas
Amenable to item analysis		Generally does not provide effective feedback to correct errors in understanding
Objective nature limits bias in scoring		
Easily administered to large numbers of students		
Efficient to score either manually or via automatic means		
Limits assessment bias caused by poor writing skills		
Less influenced by guessing than true–false items		

Adapted from *Effective multiple-choice items,* by B. J. Mandernach, 2003c. Retrieved July 7, 2006, from www.park.edu/cetl/quicktips/multiple.html

The stem. The stem establishes a problem in the mind of the test taker. Therefore, it is important that the stem itself is not ambiguous, resulting in a test taker being needlessly led astray by semantics. Consider the two stems in Figure 6.3. You'll see that the stem significantly influences students' understanding of the task at hand.

We were reminded of this while proctoring a middle school math exam. Luis, an English language learner classified as a "beginner," read the instructions that said, "Find x." He raised his hand to get our attention. He pointed to his paper where the letter x was circled and asked, "Like this?"

Figure 6.3	Examples of Stems for a Multiple-Choice Item

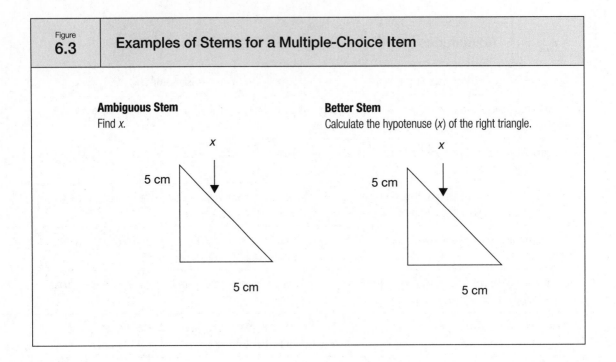

Ambiguous Stem
Find *x*.

Better Stem
Calculate the hypotenuse (*x*) of the right triangle.

Stems may be written as either direct questions or incomplete statements. An example of a direct question format looks like this:

Which of the following insects has a pupa stage in its metamorphosis?

The incomplete statement form would read:

An example of an insect that has a pupa stage is _____.

The response options. Obviously, the first rule to a good multiple-choice question is that only one answer can be correct. This doesn't mean that *all of the above* and *none of the above* cannot be used as a response option. However, it is critical that each response option is scrupulously evaluated for accuracy. Be certain to pay attention to the grammatical structures of the response options, as errors in syntax can confuse students and result in incorrect answers that are the product of poor construction, rather than a lack of understanding.

Distractors are more difficult to write than the correct answer, and it is not uncommon to see poorly constructed multiple-choice questions that contain at least one response option that is simply preposterous. This is a lost opportunity,

Figure 6.4	Multiple-Choice Item with Distractors

Stem: A plant is able to grow larger because

A. it gets its food from the soil.	Misconception	A student who chooses this answer does not understand that nutrients are manufactured internally by the plant.
B. it turns water and air into sugar.	Oversimplification	The student understands that food is manufactured internally, but does not understand that water and carbon dioxide (from the air) are used to make sugar and oxygen.
C. it has chlorophyll to produce food.	Overgeneralization	The student does not understand that some parasitic plants do not contain chlorophyll.
D. it adds biomass through photosynthesis.	Correct answer	

as well as an indication that the person who constructed the test does not have an understanding of what students know and do not know. The best distractors address misconceptions, oversimplifications, and overgeneralizations that students may possess about the topic. This is different from a simple wrong answer, which is likely to be recognized by most students as coming from left field. When distractors are developed with misconceptions in mind, teachers and students can pinpoint what is understood and not understood. They become diagnostic distractors and allow for teaching with precision (see Chapter 7 for more information on using diagnostic distractors to make teaching decisions). Consider the example in Figure 6.4.

Selection of any one of the incorrect answers (A, B, or C) yields information about what the student does not know as well as what he or she does know. Additionally, none of the choices is so far askew that it serves no purpose other than to increase the probability that a test taker can guess correctly. Notice that the example does not unnecessarily give away the correct answer by using absolutes like "never" and "always" (test-wise students know these are usually incorrect). Savvy students also anticipate that correct answers are significantly shorter or longer than the distractors. If you use a noticeably shorter or longer response option, consider making it a distractor.

A great resource for test creation, regardless of the format, is www.easytestmaker. com. This website allows you to enter the test items and will format it for you. There are services on the website that cost a nominal fee, but the test maker program is free.

Short Answer

Short-answer and completion items are both forms of "supply" items in which students have to provide the response, rather than selecting one from a teacher-generated list (as in a multiple-choice item). Short-answer test items (also called completion, supplied-response, or constructed-response items) are those that can be answered by a word, phrase, number, or symbol (Linn & Miller, 2005). They are generally considered effective as a measure of students' ability to accurately recall specific information. Short-answer items require that students either complete a statement (fill-in-the-blank or completion items) or answer a direct question using a single word or brief phrase. The advantages and disadvantages of short-answer items are presented in Figure 6.5.

Instructional objectives that require students to know certain information (e.g., those that suggest that the student recall, label, name, list, state, define, or describe) can be measured with short-answer or completion items. There are a number of common formats for these supply-type items; teachers must consider the following issues when making a decision about which format to use.

The blank line. One decision required for the use of short-answer or completion items concerns the blank line. Does the student write on the line or in another designated place? (Remember, the directions about this should be clear.) In the first example below, the student writes his or her response on the blank line at the end of the sentence. In the second example below, the student writes his or her response on the blank line to the right of the sentence:

Hydrogen has an atomic number of _____.

Hydrogen has an atomic number of _____.   _____

Specificity. Another decision to make is the degree of specificity required in student responses. A potential problem with supply-type items is that a student may provide an answer that is technically correct but not the answer the teacher wanted. If you want specific information to be provided by the student, the question can prompt for it. In the first example below, there is a range of possible

Figure 6.5	Advantages and Disadvantages of Short-Answer Items	
Advantages		**Disadvantages**
Scores less likely to be influenced by guessing		Accuracy of assessment may be influenced by handwriting/ spelling skills
Requires increased cognitive ability to generate answers		Subjective nature can make scoring difficult and time-consuming
Provides diagnostic information when looking at types of errors		Difficult to write items so that desired knowledge is clear
Promotes more in-depth study because students must recall answers		May overestimate learning due to bluffing
Effective for assessing who, what, where, and when information		Generally limited to knowledge and comprehension questions
Relatively easy to construct		Not suitable for item analysis
Effective as either a written or oral assessment		Often criticized for encouraging rote memorization
Quicker for students to complete than multiple-choice questions		

Adapted from *Developing short answer items*, by B. J. Mandernach, 2003b. Retrieved July 7, 2006, from www.park.edu/cetl/quicktips/shortanswer.html

responses that would work. In the second example below, it is clearer that the teacher is looking for a specific date (recall):

World War II started in _____.
World War II started in the year _____.

Hidden clues. Another problem with supply-type items is that the answers can sometimes be deduced from the way in which the question is written. For example, a definition may be included in the item, or the grammar structure provides the student with an unintended clue (e.g., plural version, gender, *a/an*). In the example below, the question contains an unintended clue to the answer because there simply aren't very many punctuation marks that start with a vowel:

The correct punctuation mark in sentence #4 is an _____.

Cloze procedure. In addition to using supply-type items on tests, educators can use them for reading assessments. The Cloze procedure is a technique in which words are deleted from a passage according to a word-count formula. The passage is presented to students, who insert words as they read to complete the text and construct meaning from it. This procedure can be used as a diagnostic reading assessment technique, to determine a student's independent reading level, and to check for understanding of content-area texts. It is especially helpful for content-area teachers who want to know if their reading assignments are too difficult for students or who want to check for understanding of a specific piece of text. The procedure for conducting a Cloze activity is fairly simple (McKenna & Robinson, 1980):

1. Select a piece of text and determine the grade level of the text (this can be done with the Fry Readability Formula or any number of published measures).
2. From this piece of text, select a representative 100-word passage.
3. Leave the first and last sentences and all of the punctuation intact.
4. Delete every fifth word of the remaining sentences. Replace these words with blank lines. Attempt to make all of the blank lines an equal length to avoid including visual clues about the lengths of omitted words.
5. Ask the student to read the entire passage and then reread the passage while writing in the missing words. No time limits are set.
6. Responses are correct even if misspelled, and each correct response is worth 2 points.
7. Score the assessment as follows: 57–100 points indicates an *independent* reading level for the student, 44–56 points indicates that this is the *instructional* level for the student, and less than 44 points indicates that the material is in the student's *frustrational* level (Shanker & Ekwall, 2003).

Once the results are tallied, you will have a general idea of where to begin instruction in this or a similar text. By examining the types of errors a student makes, you can determine the student's success in comprehending the passage as well as the instructional needs the specific student has.

Dichotomous Choices

Dichotomous-choice items, known commonly as true-or-false, can also be called alternative-response items or binary-choice items (Chatterji, 2003; Linn & Miller,

2005). Students are asked to identify if a declarative statement is true or false, if they agree or disagree, if it's right or wrong, if it's correct or incorrect, if it's a fact or opinion, or simply reply yes or no. The most common use of dichotomous choices is to determine if students understand the correctness of statements of fact, if they agree with opinions, if they can define terms, or if they can understand a principle. Advantages and disadvantages of dichotomous-choice items are listed in Figure 6.6.

To be most effective in assessing specific learning objectives, dichotomous-choice tests should target only one fact per item. Doing so allows the teacher to determine whether or not the students understand the particular fact, idea, principle, or opinion.

In his U.S. history class, Robert Villarino uses weekly true/false tests to check for understanding. However, to increase the cognitive demand he places on his students, Mr. Villarino requires that students correct the false items. This requires

Figure 6.6	Advantages and Disadvantages of Dichotomous-Choice Items	
Advantages		**Disadvantages**
Relatively easy to write and develop		May overestimate learning due to the influence of guessing
Quick to score		Difficult to differentiate between effective difficult items and trick items
Objective nature limits bias in scoring		Often leads to testing of trivial facts or bits of information
Easily administered to large numbers of students		Generally less discriminating than multiple-choice items
Effective as either a written or oral assessment		May not accurately reflect realistic circumstances in which issues are not absolutely true or false
Limits bias due to poor writing and/or reading skills		Often criticized for encouraging rote memorization
Highly efficient as large amount of knowledge can be sampled in a short amount of time		
Amenable to item analysis, which allows for improvement of the assessment device		

From *Quality true–false items,* by B. J. Mandernach, 2003d. Retrieved July 7, 2006, from www.park.edu/cetl/quicktips/truefalse.html

students to move beyond the simple judgment of true or false and identify specific errors within the statement to demonstrate their understanding of the information. For example, on one of his weekly tests, Mr. Villarino wrote:

> Francis Scott Key, the writer of the "Star Spangled Banner," was a supporter of the War of 1812. TRUE/FALSE

Jessica got the question right by selecting false. However, that could have been a lucky guess. Her writing confirmed that she understood the information:

> Mr. Key said that this war (1812) was "a lump of wickedness" so, unless he is very sarcastic, he did not support the war.

Importantly, studies of dichotomous-choice items suggest that students tend to mark "true" when guessing; thus, false items tend to discriminate better between students who understand the information and those who do not. Having said that, we also know that students look for patterns in tests, consciously and subconsciously, so we caution you to balance the number of questions that are true with the number that are false.

Essays

Essay items, also known as extended-response items, are the most common type of performance assessment or task we ask students to complete (Linn & Miller, 2005). The essay requires that students consolidate their understanding of a topic, organize their thinking, and present it. While essays should not be overused, they do provide an opportunity for students to synthesize or evaluate information and are thus an excellent opportunity for teachers to check for understanding. A list of advantages and disadvantages of essay items can be found in Figure 6.7.

As Criswell and Criswell (2004) note:

> Assessment reforms of the early '90s encouraged the development and use of "newer" forms of assessment including portfolios, performance tasks, and authentic assessments. As of late, however, there appears to be a regressive emphasis toward the use of objective item formats, especially in the area of state-mandated testing (Darling-Hammond, 2003). Despite shifts in assessment theory, the essay item format remained a credible and fundamental tool for assessing student achievement. (p. 510)

Figure 6.7	Advantages and Disadvantages of Essay Questions	
Advantages		**Disadvantages**
Encourage the organization of knowledge, integration of theories, and expression of opinions		Subjective scoring is less reliable, more time-consuming, and subject to bias
Promote original, novel thinking		Grading may be influenced by handwriting, length of response, and writing skills
Advantageous for assessing complex learning outcomes such as application, synthesis, and evaluation levels of understanding		Not effective in testing isolated facts or other lower-level cognitive objectives
Emphasize the ability to effectively communicate knowledge in a coherent fashion		More time-consuming to answer, so limited content can be assessed
Relatively easy to construct		May overestimate learning due to the influence of bluffing
Stimulate increased studying as students cannot answer via simple recognition		
Students are less likely to correctly guess answers without some prior knowledge		

Adapted from *Developing essay items,* by B. J. Mandernach, 2003a. Retrieved July 7, 2006, from www.park.edu/cetl/quicktips/essay.html

The essay endures because it is helpful in checking for understanding and allowing students to consolidate their thinking.

In terms of general guidelines for the development of essay items, teachers are cautioned to note the amount of time required to grade and carefully evaluate student work. While there are a number of computerized programs being developed to help teachers score essays, some of which are getting fairly reliable (Koul, Clariana, & Salehi, 2005), checking for understanding and linking assessment findings with instruction require that teachers understand the thinking of students.

In addition, there is evidence that essay grading is somewhat subjective (Blok, 1985; Wang, 2000). Sometimes subjectivity is introduced because the item is ambiguous or open to significant personal interpretation. To address this area of bias, teachers must construct items carefully and ensure that there is sufficient focus to the question.

Another way subjectivity is introduced involves the administration of the item. Students need to understand the time limits for the item, the weighting of each item (how much of the grade it is worth), and the scoring criteria that will be used. As with all types of rubrics, developing the scoring criteria with students and ensuring that students understand the criteria before participating in the assessment will result in a more accurate picture of their knowledge and allow the teacher to use this information to check for understanding (Skillings & Ferrell, 2000).

A final concern in terms of the subjectivity and bias in essay tests involves the prior knowledge the teacher has about the student and whether or not the teacher can hold that information in check while reading and scoring a specific piece of writing. Teachers can reduce this "halo effect" by grading essays without knowing the identity of the student. Some teachers fold over the corner of the front page and then mix up the papers; others implement a coding system to ensure that they are not biased in their review.

Ninth grade English teacher Chip Stroehlein's students study big ideas and essential questions. The books they read are connected to these bigger ideas. Mr. Stroehlein reads one book aloud to the class that he selects based on the theme or big idea. Students in his classes choose books connected with the theme and then read and discuss these books in literature circles. This allows Mr. Stroehlein to differentiate reading materials and meet student needs while also ensuring that the entire class is able to have a conversation on a bigger idea that matters.

During a unit titled "Is freedom ever free?" Mr. Stroehlein's students read several pieces of text, including Chief Joseph's surrender speech. Following their reading and discussion of the text, students were asked to write in response to the following prompt:

> What is the role of courage in surrender? After reading and discussing Chief Joseph's speech "I Will Fight No More Forever," write an essay that defines courage and explains the courageousness of Chief Joseph's decision. Support your discussion with evidence from the text. What conclusions can you draw?

Gilbert's response can be found in Figure 6.8. Mr. Stroehlein noted that Gilbert's use of language is sophisticated and that he defines courage and analyzes the text, noting that it took courage to surrender. The website www.literacydesigncollaborative.org

Figure 6.8	Gilbert's Response

Gilbert Garcia

Courage is weaving through a jungle weilding nothing but a gun and bow fully aware that this time youre fighting for more than just yourself. Courage is waving your hand high to be called on not even sure if your answer is right. Courage is when you do something out of your comfort zone for the greater good. When Chief Joseph wrote "I Will Fight No More" it took him a lot of courage. The Courage to speak how he felt, the courage to admit defeat, and the courage to ~~live on after~~ his decision. do what he felt was right. This poem itself is courageous.

After battling for days and maybe even months, Chief Joseph has the courage to admit defeat. "Hear me, my cheifs, I am tired. My heart is sad and sick. From where the sun now stands, I will fight no more forever." Chief Joseph summons a lot of bravery to admit his defeat to not only his opponents but his well-respected Chiefs who he looks up to himself. He also speaks his true feelings about this war instead of locking it away and continuing to fight a pointless war.

provides templates that teachers can use in developing writing prompts that require evidence from the text.

Tips for Success

As Tomlinson (1999) so aptly states, "Assessment always has more to do with helping students grow than with cataloging their mistakes" (p. 11). We couldn't agree more. Tests and assessments can and should be used to check for understanding with the goal of increasingly precise instruction for individual students. Although we acknowledge that tests and assessments will be used for other purposes—report cards, grading, and public accountability, to name a few—it is critical that we also use the information we gather through testing to plan our instruction.

Some tips to consider as you use tests to check for understanding include the following:

• Talk about the role of tests with students and help them understand that there are different tests used for different reasons. Focus some instructional time on test-taking strategies and understanding the genre of different tests.
• Consider the benefits and drawbacks of each test type, and match the type of test with the information you need to check for understanding. Make sure students understand the test-taking procedures for each type of assessment.
• Develop diagnostic distractors for test items with distractors so that each incorrect response teaches you something about students' understanding.
• Use tests formatively, as well as summatively, to guide future instruction and intervention efforts.

7

Using Common Formative Assessments to Check for Understanding

When teachers in course-alike groups or grade-level teams meet on a regular basis to look at student work, checking for understanding becomes a systemwide process. Like the authors of *Collaborative Analysis of Student Work* (Langer, Colton, & Goff, 2003) and *Common Formative Assessments* (Ainsworth & Viegut, 2006), in this chapter we explore the ways that teacher teams can use assessment information to guide their instructional interventions. We also describe ways in which teachers can use common formative assessments to increase their expectations, tune the curriculum, and inform instruction.

Using Data to Improve Student Achievement

There are a number of strategies that can be used to improve student achievement and close the achievement gap, including hiring veteran teachers, purchasing new curricula, providing after-school tutoring, and so on. These are all likely to have positive effects on the achievement of students who are performing at less than acceptable levels. Our experience, however, suggests that it is the teacher and what the teacher does that make the difference for students (Frey & Fisher, 2006). We know that access to professional development differentiates teachers who have the knowledge and skills to meet the increasing demands of our diverse student population and those who do not (Joyce & Showers, 2002). We also know that not all professional development is created equally (National Staff Development Council, 2001). Teachers deserve professional development that is engaging, based on current research evidence, aligned with standards, and provides them opportunities for peer engagement.

Understanding this, we have developed and implemented a protocol for examining and aligning content standards, creating common assessments, scoring student work by consensus, and planning changes based on the information gathered in this process. Let's explore the protocol first and then look at the results of the protocol in checking for understanding and in closing the achievement gap.

A Protocol for Using Common Assessments

A number of recursive steps can be used to align curriculum, instruction, and assessment such that student learning becomes the focus of professional development and teachers can check for understanding at the grade or department level. A record-keeping tool for this process can be found in Figure 7.1.

Step 1: Pacing Guides

The first step in the process involves gathering teachers with common courses (e.g., 3rd grade, 7th grade English, U.S. history, algebra) to meet and decide on a timeline for the sequence of content instruction. The group of teachers will need access to their content standards to ensure that each standard is addressed in a meaningful way. While this sounds easy, it can be the most difficult part of the protocol. Some teachers may resist standards-aligned instruction; others may have their favorite units or teaching order. Still others may be unfamiliar with their content standards and the expectations of their specific grade level. It is hard to imagine a way to close the achievement gap if students do not have access to instruction that is aligned with the grade-level standards.

Step 2: Instructional Materials and Arrangements

Once pacing guides have been agreed upon, teachers must select instructional materials, strategies, approaches, and arrangements. While the materials may be selected for teachers in many states, they know that they can use the materials in a

FIGURE 7.1	Tools for Implementing the Common Assessment Protocol

Weekly Course-Alike Meeting

Course:	Date:

Lead teacher or facilitator:

Teachers in attendance:

Focus: (indicate one)
Curriculum pacing guide
Strategy implementation
Coaching practice
Consensus scoring cycle
    Common assessment development
    Item analysis (See reverse side. Do not complete remainder of this page.)

Discussion points:	Questions raised:
Objective for the coming week:	**Resources needed:**

Implementation steps:

(continued)

FIGURE 7.1	Tools for Implementing the Common Assessment Protocol (*continued*)

Item Analysis Summary

Assessment tool:

Student work: Areas of strength

Student work: Areas of weakness

Teacher practice: What should be preserved?

Teacher practice: Identify gaps between existing and desired practice.

Teacher practice: What aspects of existing practice pose a barrier to implementing desired practice?

Teacher practice: Suggested interventions or unit modifications

Unanswered questions:

Adapted by R. Elwardi and L. Mongrue from *Smaller learning communities: Implementing and deepening practice*, by D. Oxley, 2005, Portland, OR: Northwest Regional Educational Laboratory.

variety of ways. In discussions during this step in the protocol, teachers share their evidence-based and effective instructional approaches with one another. In addition, the team may request assistance from a consultant who has more information about instructional strategies and approaches. In this way, the work of the consultant is contextualized in the work of the teacher teams.

Step 3: Common Assessments

At predetermined points in the school year, but no less than every six weeks, students should participate in a common assessment of their learning. While there are a number of commercially available tests and assessments, our experience suggests that when groups of teachers create their own common assessments, scores rise faster. Creating an assessment, even an imperfect one, allows groups of teachers to talk about the standards, how the standards might be assessed, where students are performing currently, and what learning needs to take place for students to demonstrate proficiency. In other words, creating common assessments provides teachers with an opportunity to "begin with the end in mind" (Covey, 2004). In addition, common assessments provide students with test format practice, which has been documented to increase performance (Langer, 2001). When students understand the genre of the test, they are likely to do better.

Step 4: Consensus Scoring and Item Analysis

Once all of the students have participated in the common assessment and the results have been tabulated, teachers should meet to discuss the results. The results are presented for the grade or course, not for individual teachers. The results are also disaggregated by significant subpopulations, such as students with disabilities, students who are English language learners, or specific ethnic/racial groups. This allows teachers to identify and discuss achievement gaps and plan interventions.

When considering a specific item, teachers note the number or percentage of students who answered correctly and hypothesize why the students who answered incorrectly did so. They question one another about students' understandings and misunderstandings and theorize about future instruction, pacing, instructional materials, assessments, and planning.

Step 5: Revising Pacing Guides, Reviewing Assessments, Reteaching, and Forming Intervention Groups

As teachers review student work, they note changes that need to be made in the pacing guides, review standards for clarification of the content, and plan for reteaching opportunities. Teachers also discuss the implications that specific instructional materials have for students' learning and make recommendations about changes in this aspect. In some schools, teachers request the assessment data for their own students so that they can compare with the school, department, or grade average. This final step provides an opportunity for the protocol to cycle again; the assessment data inform instruction, curriculum, and future assessments. Along the way, gaps in student performance are identified and plans are developed to address these gaps, whether they be between ethnic/racial groups or between the students and the state content standards. The teacher may choose to meet with certain groups of students on a temporary basis, providing instruction on the missing subject knowledge or skills. In high-performing schools, gaps in student knowledge are often addressed in after-school programs such as the federally funded 21st Century Community Learning Centers. Thus, common assessments become the link between the school day and the after-school interventions.

The Protocol in Action

The protocol was used by a group of five teachers who all teach the same course. The teachers met regularly to discuss their content standards and the ways in which those content standards can be assessed. They regularly administer a common assessment that includes 10 to 12 questions. They also use writing prompts and interviews to explore students' thinking about the content. On a recent common assessment, the following question was used:

For what purpose did Parliament vote during the Restoration?

A. To restore Puritan religion in England

B. To restore the monarchy in England

C. To restore Charles I to power

D. To restore the idea of the divine right of kings

In terms of responses, 37.5 percent of the students chose A, 7.5 percent chose B (the correct answer), 17.5 percent chose C, and 37.5 percent chose D. While we might debate the relative merit of the question or the importance of this point in the overall understanding of history, the teachers noted that this is the type of question that confuses students on the state assessment and that this type of question is commonly asked of students on these assessments.

Having acknowledged this result, the conversation that the teachers had about this one question illustrates the power of this process. One of the teachers explained, "Restoration is when they brought the king back. I never really discussed the fact that Parliament voted on this. I really focus on the timeline, not so much why. Using the timeline, my students know that Oliver Cromwell ruined arts and literature and that Charles II restored them. I think that I missed one of the keys here, that Parliament restored the monarchy and ended the military dictatorship."

Another teacher focused on students' seeming lack of test-taking skills. He said, "Our students should have been able to delete several items right away. Charles I was beheaded, so C can't be right. Also, the divine right of kings is a belief system, not something that Parliament could or could not restore. They should have crossed those two choices off right away. We have to go back and review some common test-taking skills."

Maria Grant is a science teacher who regularly facilitates conversations with her colleagues about student work. A sample question from a recent biology common formative assessment can be found in Figure 7.2. Based on student response to this item, the teachers had the following conversation.

Mr. Simms encouragingly reported, "The greatest percentage of students did choose the correct answer." Ms. Jackson quickly curbed the group's enthusiasm by noting, "Fifty-four percent of the students didn't choose the right answer." She added, "Seventeen percent chose answer A. This might mean that students don't understand how to determine percentages. I think that we should all do a quick review of some basic skills. Who can develop a quick review for us all to use?"

Mr. Simms offered to develop the review and then added, "Though I covered the main concepts of Mendelian genetics, it seems that students didn't really understand how expressed traits are passed from parent to offspring." Mrs. Rodriguez agreed, "Yes, and 11 percent chose answer B. The students who chose this answer

FIGURE 7.2	**Sample Biology Question and Results**

In a certain species of insect, the allele for brown eyes (B) is dominant to the allele for blue eyes (b). For this species, eye color does not depend on the sex of the organism. When a team of scientists decided to cross a male and a female that both had brown eyes, they found that 31 offspring had brown eyes and 9 had blue eyes. What are the *most likely* genotypes of the parent insects?

    A. BB and bb
    B. bb and bb
    C. Bb and Bb
    D. BB and Bb

What the students chose:
    A. 17%
    B. 11%
    C. 46% (correct answer)
    D. 26%

don't seem to understand the concept of a dominant allele. Maybe I need to focus more on vocabulary instruction for this group of students. We had the key terms, but they don't seem to know how to use them. In addition to the math review, I think we should find out the specific students who missed this and get to them during small-group time."

Ms. Jackson also noted, "I think we need to work on test-taking skills. Our students should have been able to eliminate answers A and B right away because each shows a parent with blue eyes, and the question states that both parents have brown eyes." Mr. Simms added, "Twenty-six percent of our students chose answer D. Maybe they thought that since three out of four alleles are B, there's a correlation to the 31 out of 40 total species with brown eyes as described in the question. I think I need to review how to use Punnet's squares."

Ms. Grant asked the group if they thought that sharing the item analysis with students might also facilitate their thinking about the content. As she said, "What if we showed all of the students this item analysis and asked them to work in small groups to determine why specific answers were wrong? Wouldn't that help them understand the test as a genre and get them test format practice?" Mr. Simms agreed, noting that this would also be teaching biology and not simply test practice.

Christine Johnson is a teacher and the facilitator of the course-alike conversations in history. This history department has piloted a metacognitive task in combination with the content knowledge task. For each question that students answer, they also indicated one of the following four choices:

- I knew it
- I figured it out
- I guessed at it
- I don't care

For example, during a discussion the group started their conversation about a question that troubled a number of students (see Figure 7.3). As Mr. Jacobs said, "Let's start with question 3. Only 61 percent of the students got it right and only

FIGURE 7.3	Sample History Questions and Results

3. In a(n) _____, all citizens at mass meetings make decisions for the government.
   a. monarchy
   b. oligarchy
   c. direct democracy
   d. representative democracy

10. Use the map below to answer the following question: Sparta is located _____ of Athens.
    a. northwest
    b. northeast
    c. southwest
    d. southeast

3. What the students chose:
   a. 7%
   b. 2%
   c. 61% (correct answer)
   d. 30%

10. What the students chose:
    a. 10%
    b. 3%
    c. 58% (correct answer)
    d. 29%

38 percent of them self-reported that they knew it. According to the same self-assessment, an additional 36 percent had 'figured it out' and 24 percent indicated that they 'guessed at it.' It's interesting that only 3 kids (of 241) didn't care about this question. I know that I taught this. But most of the wrong answers were still based on democracy, but not the right type of democracy. I think this could be a quick fix. We need to make sure that students really have a sense of the difference between direct and representative democracy. I have an idea for a simulation that could really solidify this for students." Mr. Jacobs proceeded to describe his idea for a simulation and the teachers agreed to reteach this idea.

From the students' self-assessment, the teachers determined a correlation between correctness and a confident response in "knowing" the answer. Also, accuracy was evident in the "figuring it out" indicator. The teachers were pleased to see that the students were using their test-taking strategies of elimination or using context clues.

Mrs. Johnson then turned their attention to question 10 when she said, "Here we go again. Our students still don't have a sense of the cardinal points. We keep asking them questions that require them to use map skills, but they are getting them wrong. Look here, just over 50 percent correct. We have to focus on interpreting maps every day. It's not just about using this for history and geography. This is a life skill." Ms. Vasquez confessed, "I don't really know how to teach this. I've shown my students the map and the directions. I don't know what to do differently so that they learn this." Mrs. Johnson suggested that Ms. Vasquez visit another teacher's class and observe. As Mrs. Johnson said, "I'll cover your class so that you can go observe Mr. Applegate. Is that okay? Then we can talk further about reteaching the concept of cardinal points. Does anyone else need help with this? Only half of our students are getting this!" Mrs. Johnson also suggested that the group consider revising the pacing guide to allow for more time to teach map skills. The group continued to analyze the results and in the process identified a small group of students who would benefit from instruction to build their background knowledge. These students were found to have missed all of the items related to government structures, and the group suspected that they lacked background knowledge. Mr. Applegate met with them during the school's after-school program, where students who need additional intervention are tutored.

To check for their students' understanding using this protocol, a group of 3rd grade teachers analyzed individual items on a common assessment. First, they correlated the items with content standards and identified items aligned with key standards that fewer than 60 percent of students answered correctly. Next, they identified items aligned with nonkey standards that had fewer than 60 percent correct responses. There were four key standards and seven nonkey standards associated with items that fewer than 60 percent of students got correct. The teachers then checked to see how many questions were asked for each standard and considered each question on the test for discussion.

Using the standards analysis, the teachers discovered that the key standard with the lowest percent correct was in the area of measurement and geometry. Standard MG 1.3 reads, "Find the perimeter of a polygon with integer sides." There were two items on the assessment that addressed this standard: one item showed a rectangle with the length and width labeled, and the second item showed a rectangle with squares filled in and no measurements given. Although 76.6 percent of the students selected the correct answer for the first item, only 28.9 percent answered the second item correctly. Even more puzzling was the fact that 48.1 percent of the students chose the same incorrect response to the second item. Figure 7.4 shows this second item.

The teachers determined that the question was valid and simply stated. The next step was to look at the distractors. It soon became apparent to the teachers that the students who chose C (48.1 percent) were most likely trying to find the *area* by counting the squares or multiplying 5 by 6 and chose the answer 29 because it was closest to the area (30 sq ft). Another suggestion was that when the students saw the grid with all the little squares, they immediately thought of area since that is how they usually see the area questions presented in the text. The teachers were still confused as to why the students had a difficult time finding the perimeter. After much discussion, the group came to the consensus that they really needed to work on teaching perimeter in various ways, especially when a grid is given with no values.

In a similar fashion, a group of 5th grade teachers analyzed common math assessment items and also spent a great deal of time unpacking the curriculum and revising the pacing guide. The 5th grade teachers found that there were five key standards in which fewer than 60 percent of students selected the correct choice; of those five, four were in the area of measurement and geometry. This was of great concern to the teachers because it was apparent that it was a weak area. Let's

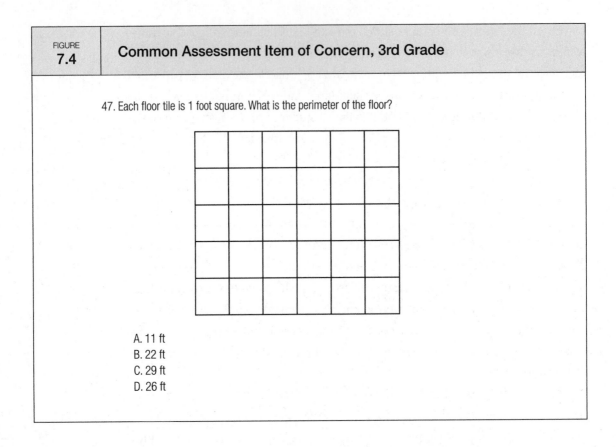

| FIGURE 7.4 | Common Assessment Item of Concern, 3rd Grade |

47. Each floor tile is 1 foot square. What is the perimeter of the floor?

A. 11 ft
B. 22 ft
C. 29 ft
D. 26 ft

consider an item representing key standard MG 1.2: "Construct a cube and rectangular box from two-dimensional patterns and use these patterns to compute the surface area for these objects." See Figure 7.5.

The interesting thing about this problem is that 22.7 percent of the students chose answer A, 23.8 percent chose C, and 42.7 percent chose D (the correct response). The teachers were at a loss to explain how the students came up with a response of 16 units, but they guessed that some students chose 4 units because they added (or multiplied) the 2 units and 2 units that were on the illustration. The group felt that the question was valid but wondered if there was too much information given, confusing the students. Determining what information is needed to solve a problem was definitely a strategy that needed emphasis. The 5th grade teachers also agreed that they needed to do more work with surface area in general.

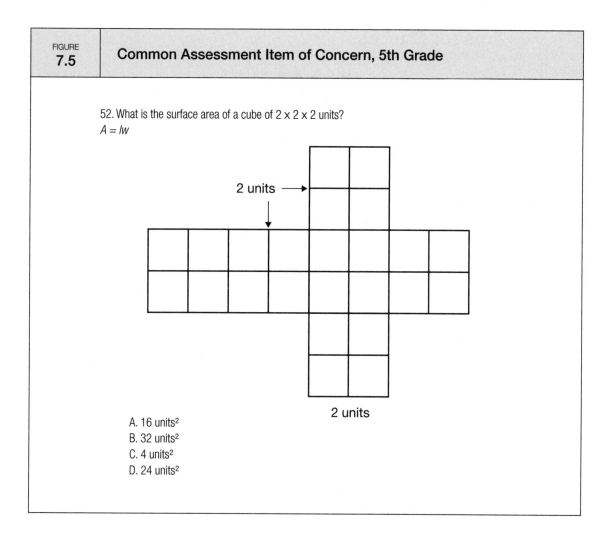

FIGURE 7.5 — Common Assessment Item of Concern, 5th Grade

52. What is the surface area of a cube of 2 x 2 x 2 units?

$A = lw$

2 units →

2 units

A. 16 units²
B. 32 units²
C. 4 units²
D. 24 units²

In the fall of each school year, an all-day meeting is held for each grade level to discuss only mathematics. At that meeting, data regarding common assessments are distributed to the teachers and time is taken to evaluate test items and to work on strategies for teaching difficult concepts. If teachers did not have all the data on each item and were not given the time to compare the data and examine the items in question, they would never really know what their students understood or how they could better instruct their students. The teachers at all grade levels have expressed how much they value the time to meet and discuss their grade-level content.

Tips for Success

Creating systems for teachers to engage with their peers and administrators in systematically looking at student work, supported with collaboratively developed pacing guides and common assessments, can help close the achievement gap that has persisted for decades. We do not need to change teachers to get the results our students deserve. Instead, we need to focus our professional development on ensuring that teachers understand their grade-level and content-specific standards, how those standards are assessed, and what to do when students do not perform well.

Some tips to consider as you use common formative assessments to check for understanding include the following:

- Dig deeply into, and develop a sophisticated understanding of, the content standards so that appropriate common formative assessments can be developed.
- Develop common formative assessments in collaboration with your peers. Some of the best professional development occurs when groups of teachers attempt to create assessment items from the standards.
- Analyze student responses collaboratively. In doing so, you'll likely gain greater understanding of students' thinking, which you can use later in your instruction.
- Use this as a recursive and continuous process rather than a single event. This type of checking for understanding should become part of the regular operation of the grade level, department, and school.

Afterword:
Checking Your Own Understanding

This book has been about checking students' understanding as they learn. But it is also about the implications of checking for understanding on our own classroom and schoolwide practices, especially with regard to reflective teaching and collaboration with our colleagues. To borrow a term from Wiggins and McTighe, we offer a few of our own "enduring understandings" about the process as it relates to teaching, learning, and school reform efforts.

Checking for Understanding Fosters Good Teaching

The most immediate benefit of checking for understanding in the classroom is that it results in improved teaching. Old (and ineffective) habits associated with relying on an Initiate-Respond-Evaluate cycle of questioning are supplanted when teachers use questioning to determine what is known and unknown. Students' verbal and written responses are valued because they provide a window into the minds of learners by answering the teacher's perpetual question: What is the next instructional move?

Teachers who regularly check for understanding appreciate the need to get responses from all students, not just the ones who know the answer. After all, this process makes it clear that understanding can't be adequately checked when only a few responses are considered. In too many classrooms, a tacit agreement between teacher and students is maintained: I'll ask the questions, a few of you will answer for the entire class, and we'll all pretend this is the same as learning. A teacher who checks for understanding seeks responses from students who do not commonly raise their hands. Checking for understanding means viewing work samples, providing opportunities for performance, and broadening the definition of testing and assessment beyond a grade-giving function.

Checking for Understanding Fosters Metacognition

When teachers become more deliberate in the ways they check for understanding, they model the metacognitive awareness learners need to develop. Metacognition is the ability of learners to "predict their performances on various tasks . . . and to monitor their current levels of mastery and understanding" (National Research Council, 2000, p. 12). While it may appear that checking for understanding is a teacher-centered strategy, in truth, it empowers students to take responsibility for their own learning through monitoring and goal setting. When teachers make checking for understanding a routine part of the learning environment, they demonstrate the many ways in which to recognize that learning has occurred. Importantly, the teacher who checks for understanding transmits the message that the goal of the classroom is not just to get a good grade but also to learn (National Research Council, 2000).

Checking for Understanding Encourages Looking for Multiple Representations of Knowledge

The process of checking for understanding requires that teachers move beyond asking questions and giving tests to determine whether learning has occurred. Many of the routine practices of schooling take on new possibilities in the hands of a skilled educator. Written work and projects offer evidence of the ways in which a student is learning, not just a simple measure of the volume of learning. A teacher who seeks to check for understanding creates new opportunities for students to demonstrate their learning. This teacher knows that he or she cannot just pause occasionally during a lecture to ask, "Any questions?" The teacher must ensure that students are given ways to reply in writing, such as summary writing of a key concept or developing a graphic organizer of the relationships between concepts. The teacher incorporates projects, portfolios, and performances into the routine of the classroom. Over time, students learn that there is more than one way to demonstrate their learning and more than one way to monitor their own understanding.

Checking for Understanding Deepens Assessment

In traditional classrooms, assessment is narrowly defined as a testing function. Student learning is routinely assessed summatively, with relatively little attention afforded to incremental appraisals of progress toward learning goals. Students view these events with anxiety, knowing that they need to perform well in order to earn a good grade. The world is thus divided into right and wrong answers, and learning is equated with the ability to memorize, recall, and regurgitate information on demand.

In classrooms where assessment and testing are used to check for understanding, teachers are clear about the purposes for these events. Students come to expect that their teachers will regularly ask them about what they know so far in order to make instructional decisions. In departments and grade levels where common assessments are given, learners hear the language of reflective teaching. They know their teachers will meet to discuss the results of the assessments and talk about instruction. It is possible that in such classrooms, students will hear their teachers explain why they are teaching the lesson and what they hope to accomplish. Because teachers who use common assessments collaborate to create these measures, they develop greater clarity about their purposes for teaching and how understanding can be assessed.

Checking for Understanding Is Aligned with Best Practices

A final advantage in checking for understanding is that it is aligned with many of the best practices associated with planning, instruction, and school reform. First, checking for understanding demands that one knows what is worth checking. As Wiggins and McTighe (2005) note, understanding is more than just "knowing" something; it is the ability to apply what is known to a new situation or task. Checking for understanding ultimately involves knowing what the enduring understandings of a lesson should be and what knowledge, skills, and strategies are needed to progress to that level. Planning, then, necessarily includes the learning that will be assessed and the methods that best accomplish that learning.

Checking for understanding is critical to differentiating instruction (Tomlinson, 1999). In a differentiated classroom, content, process, and product are aligned to student strengths and needs, allowing each learner to operate in an optimal learning environment. Therefore, the teacher must have a clear understanding of the ways in which each student will demonstrate his or her progress toward mastery. Tomlinson compares this to conducting an orchestra, with players working on different sections of the score. The role of the teacher is to achieve a balance and harmony across the players so that those enduring understandings are achieved by all, resulting in a successful performance.

Finally, checking for understanding is consistent with school reform efforts that seek to link instruction and assessment in meaningful ways. Fullan et al.'s (2006) call for "expert systems" in schools offers clear connections to the classroom. They define expert systems as ". . . two key subsystems. One is the knowledge base about what experts do in particular situations; the other is the case-specific data that relates to the situation at hand. Experts are nothing without data on current status" (p. 47). This perspective has two implications for school reform: first, with regard to what will serve as the knowledge base and the data to be examined; and second, with respect to what ways teachers and administrators will have opportunities to analyze, synthesize, and evaluate that information. Therefore, checking for understanding is useful at the school level as well as in classroom instruction. As a practice, checking for understanding should be a model for the ways in which we collaborate with our colleagues.

Checking Your Own Understanding

Tomlinson's comparison of teaching and learning to the tasks of an orchestra leader is useful when thinking about our own professional learning. Ultimately, checking for understanding is not a hierarchical or linear set of strategies and procedures. While we have arranged this book according to the constructs associated with classroom teaching, the strategies for checking for understanding become richer when considered across domains. Oral language, for instance, has everything to do with questioning, writing, and performance. In order to advance your own comprehension of checking for understanding, it is necessary to monitor your learning, reflect on its implications, and engage with colleagues in analyzing both instructional practice and the data that are yielded from such efforts. To this end, we have included a note-taking guide (see Figure A.1) for you to record your knowledge about strategies used to check for understanding. In addition, we have created an online study guide (visit www.ascd.org/studyguides) for you and your department, grade level, or school to use as you expand your efforts to check for understanding.

FIGURE A.1	Checking for Understanding Strategy Grid

1. Oral Language

Strategy	Description	How I Can Use It
Accountable talk		
Noticing nonverbal cues		
Value lineups		
Retellings		
Think-Pair-Share		
Think-Pair-Square		
Novel Ideas Only		

2. Questioning

Strategy	Description	How I Can Use It
Bloom's taxonomy		
Webb's Depth of Knowledge		
Text-dependent questions		
Response cards		
Hand signals		
Audience response systems		
ReQuest		
Socratic seminar		

3. Writing

Strategy	Description	How I Can Use It
Interactive writing		
Read-Write-Pair-Share		
Summary writing		
Writing-to-learn prompts		
RAFT		

FIGURE A.1	Checking for Understanding Strategy Grid (*continued*)

4. Projects and Performances

Strategy	Description	How I Can Use It
Readers' Theatre		
Multimedia presentations		
Electronic and paper portfolios		
Graphic organizers		
Inspiration		
Foldables		
Dioramas		
Public performances		

5. Tests

Strategy	Description	How I Can Use It
Multiple-choice items		
Short-answer items		
Dichotomous choices		
Essays		

6. Common Assessments

Strategy	Description	How I Can Use It
Pacing guides		
Instructional materials and arrangements		
Common assessments		
Consensus scoring and item analysis		
Revising pacing guides, reviewing assessments, reteaching, and forming intervention groups		

References

Adams, C. (2004). *Guidelines for participants in a Socratic seminar.* Vestivia Hills High School, Birmingham, AL.

Adler, D. A. (1992). *A picture book of Harriet Tubman.* New York: Holiday House.

Ainsworth, L., & Viegut, D. (2006). *Common formative assessments: How to connect standards-based instruction and assessment.* Thousand Oaks, CA: Corwin.

Bainton, G. (1890). *The art of authorship: Literary reminiscences, methods of work, and advice to young beginners, personally contributed by leading authors of the day.* London: J. Clark and Co.

Barron, B. (2006). Interest and self-sustained learning as catalysts of development: A learning ecology perspective. *Human Development, 49*(4), 193–224.

Barron, B. J. S., Schwartz, D. L., Vye, N. J., Moore, A., Petrosino, A., Zech, L., et al. (1998). Doing with understanding: Lessons from research on problem- and project-based learning. *Journal of the Learning Sciences, 7*(3/4), 271–311.

Beck, I., McKeown, M., Hamilton, R., & Kucan, L. (1997). *Questioning the author: An approach for enhancing student engagement with text.* Newark, DE: International Reading Association.

Black, A., & Stave, A.M. (2007). *A comprehensive guide to readers theatre: Enhancing fluency in middle school and beyond.* Newark, DE: International Reading Association.

Blok, H. (1985). Estimating the reliability, validity, and invalidity of essay ratings. *Journal of Educational Measurement, 22*(1), 41–52.

Bloom, B. S. (1956). *Taxonomy of educational objectives: The classification of educational goals: Handbook I, Cognitive domain.* New York: Longman.

Bloom, B. S., & Broder, L. J. (1950). *Problem-solving processes of college students: An exploratory investigation.* Chicago: University of Chicago Press.

Blume, J. (1972). *Tales of a fourth grade nothing.* New York: Dutton.

Britton, J. N. (1970). *Language and learning.* London: Allen Lane.

Brookhart, S. M. (2008). *How to give effective feedback to your students.* Alexandria, VA: ASCD.

Brophy, J., & Alleman, J. (2002). Learning and teaching about cultural universals in primary-grade social studies. *Elementary School Journal, 103*(2), 99–114.

Brophy, J. E., & Evertson, C. M. (1974). *Texas teacher effectiveness project: Final report.* (Research Rep. No. 74-4). Austin, TX: University of Texas.

Cambourne, B. (1998). *Read and retell.* Melbourne, Australia: Nelson.

Cazden, C. B. (1988). *Classroom discourse: The language of teaching and learning.* Portsmouth, NH: Heinemann.

Chatterji, M. (2003). *Designing and using tools for educational assessment.* Boston: Allyn and Bacon.

Christenbury, L. (2006). *Making the journey: Being and becoming a teacher of English language arts.* Portsmouth, NH: Heinemann.

Clay, M. M. (2001). *Change over time in children's literacy development.* Portsmouth, NH: Heinemann.

Cooper, P., & Morreale, S. (Eds.). (2003). *Creating competent communicators: Activities for teaching speaking, listening, and media literacy in K–6 classrooms.* Scottsdale, AZ: Holcomb Hathaway.

Costa, A. L., & Kallick, B. (Eds.). (2000). *Discovering and exploring habits of mind.* Alexandria, VA: ASCD.

Cotton, K. (1989). Expectations and student outcomes. Portland, OR: Northwest Regional Educational Laboratory. Available: www.nwrel.org/scpd/sirs/4/cu7.html

Covey, S. R. (2004). *The 7 habits of highly effective people: Powerful lessons in personal change* (Rev. ed.). New York: Free Press.

Criswell, J. R., & Criswell, S. J. (2004). Asking essay questions: Answering contemporary needs. *Education, 124,* 510–516.

Curtis, C. P. (1995). *The Watsons go to Birmingham—1963.* New York: Delacorte Press.

Darling-Hammond, L. (2003). Standards and assessments: Where we are and what we need. *Teacher's College Record.* Available: http://www.tcrecord.org/content.asp?ContentID=11109

Daywalt, D. (2013). *The day the crayons quit.* New York: Philomel Books.

dePaola, T. (1973). *Nana upstairs and Nana downstairs.* New York: Putnam.

Edens, K. M., & Potter, E. (2003). Using descriptive drawings as a conceptual change strategy in elementary science. *School Science and Mathematics, 103*(3), 135–144.

Egan, M. (1999). Reflections on effective use of graphic organizers. *Journal of Adolescent and Adult Literacy, 42,* 641–645.

Elbow, P. (1994). *Writing for learning—not just for demonstrating learning.* Retrieved July 2, 2006, from http://www.ntlf.com/html/lib/bib/writing.htm

Esch, C. (1998). Project-based and problem-based: Same or different? Retrieved July 7, 2006, from http://pblmm.k12.ca.us/PBLGuide/PBL&PBL.htm

Ferretti, R. P., MacArthur, C. D., & Okolo, C. M. (2001). Teaching for historical understanding in inclusive classrooms. *Learning Disability Quarterly, 24,* 59–71.

Fisher, D., & Frey, N. (2007). *Scaffolded writing: A gradual release approach to writing instruction.* New York: Scholastic.

Fisher, D., & Frey, N. (2010). *Guided instruction: How to develop confident and successful learners.* Alexandria, VA: ASCD.

Fisher, D., & Frey, N. (2011). *The purposeful classroom: How to structure lessons with learning goals in mind.* Alexandria, VA: ASCD.

Fisher, D., & Frey, N. (2013). *Common core English language arts in a PLC at work: Grades 6-8.* Bloomington, IN: Solution Tree.

Fisher, D., & Frey, N. (2013b). *Better learning through structured teaching: A framework for the gradual release of responsibility* (2nd ed.). Alexandria, VA: ASCD.

Fisher, D., & Johnson, C. (2006). Using data to improve student achievement. *Principal Leadership, 7*(2), 27–31.

Fisher, D., Lapp, D., & Flood, J. (2005). Consensus scoring and peer planning: Meeting literacy accountability demands one school at a time. *The Reading Teacher, 58,* 656–667.

Flanders, N. (1970). *Analyzing teaching behavior.* Reading, MA: Addison-Wesley.

Frey, N., & Fisher, D. (2006). *Language arts workshop: Purposeful reading and writing instruction.* Upper Saddle River, NJ: Pearson/Merrill/Prentice Hall.

Frey, N., & Fisher, D. (2007). *Reading for information in elementary school: Content literacy strategies to build comprehension.* Upper Saddle River, NJ: Pearson/Merrill/Prentice Hall.

Fullan, M., Hill, P., & Crévola, C. (2006). *Breakthrough.* Thousand Oaks, CA: Corwin Press.

Gardner, H. (1983). *Frames of mind: The theory of multiple intelligences.* New York: Basic Books.

Gibson, S. A. (2008). An effective framework for primary-grade guided writing lessons. *The Reading Teacher, 62*(4), 324–334.

Ginsburg, H. (1982). *Children's arithmetic: The learning process* (Rev. ed.). New York: Van Nostrand.

Gollub, M. (2000). *The jazz fly.* Santa Rosa, CA: Tortuga Press.

Gould, L. L. (2001). *America in the Progressive Era, 1890–1914.* New York: Longman.

Gould, S. J. (1981). *The mismeasure of man.* New York: Norton.

Graff, G., & Birkenstein, C. (2006). *They say / I say: The moves that matter in academic writing.* New York: W. W. Norton & Company.

Greenfader, C., & Brouillette, L. (2013). Boosting language skills of English learners through dramatization and movement. *The Reading Teacher, 67*(3), 171–180.

Guan Eng Ho, D. (2005). Why do teachers ask the questions they ask? *RELC Journal, 36,* 297–310.

Hattie, J., & Timperley, H. (2007). The power of feedback. *Review of Educational Research, 77,* 81–112.

Heward, W. L., Gardner, R., III, Cavanaugh, R. A., Courson, F. H., Grossi, T. A., & Barbetta, P. M. (1996). Everyone participates in this class: Using response cards to increase active student response. *Teaching Exceptional Children, 28*(2), 4–10.

Hmelo, C. (1998). Problem-based learning: Effects on early acquisition of cognitive skill in medicine. *Journal of the Learning Sciences, 7,* 173–208.

Hopkinson, D. (1993). *Sweet Clara and the freedom quilt.* New York: Knopf.

Hoyt, L. (2008). *Revisit, reflect, retell: Time-tested strategies for teaching reading comprehension.* Portsmouth, NH: Heinemann.

Jago, C. (2002). *Cohesive writing: Why concept is not enough.* Portsmouth, NH: Heinemann.

Johnson, D. W., & Johnson, R. (1998). Cooperative learning and social interdependence theory. In R. Tindale, L. Heath, J. Edwards, E. Posavac, F. Bryant, Y. Suzrez-Balcazar, et al. (Eds.), *Theory and research on small groups: Social psychological applications to social issues* (Vol. 4, pp. 9–36). New York: Plenum Press.

Joyce, B., & Showers, B. (2002). *Student achievement through staff development* (3rd ed.). Alexandria, VA: ASCD.

Kagan, S. (1994). *Cooperative learning.* San Clemente, CA: Kagan Press.

Kindsvatter, R., Wilen, W., & Ishler, M. (1996). *Dynamics of effective teaching* (3rd ed.). White Plains: Longman.

Kluger, A. N., & DeNisi, A. (1996). The effects of feedback interventions on performance: A historical review, a meta-analysis, and a preliminary feedback intervention theory. *Psychological Bulletin, 119*(2), 254–284.

Kohn, A. (2000). *The case against standardized testing: Raising the scores, ruining the schools.* Portsmouth, NH: Heinemann.

Koul, R., Clariana, R. B., & Salehi, R. (2005). Comparing several human and computer-based methods for scoring concept maps and essays. *Journal of Educational Computing Research, 32,* 227–239.

Kuhrt, B. L., & Farris, P. J. (1990). Empowering students through reading, writing, and reasoning. *Journal of Reading, 33,* 436–441.

Lajoie, S. (2005). Extending the scaffolding metaphor. *Instructional Science, 33,* 541–557.

Langer, G. M., Colton, A. B., & Goff, L. S. (2003). *Collaborative analysis of student work: Improving teaching and learning.* Alexandria, VA: ASCD.

Langer, J. A. (2001). Beating the odds: Teaching middle and high school students to read and write well. *American Educational Research Journal, 38,* 837–880.

Langley, A. (2005). *Ancient Egypt.* Chicago: Raintree.

Lapp, D., Fisher, D., Flood, J., & Cabello, A. (2001). An integrated approach to the teaching and assessment of language arts. In S. R. Hurley & J. V. Tinajero (Eds.), *Literacy assessment of second language learners* (pp. 1–26). Boston: Allyn & Bacon.

Lester, J. (1998). *From slave ship to Freedom Road.* New York: Dial Books.

Lingard, B., Hayes, D., & Mills, M. (2003). Teachers and productive pedagogies: Contextualising, conceptualising, utilising. *Pedagogy, Culture and Society, 11,* 399–424.

Linn, R. L., & Miller, M. D. (2005). *Measurement and assessment in teaching* (9th ed.). Upper Saddle River, NJ: Merrill Prentice Hall.

Lyman, F. T. (1981). The responsive classroom discussion: The inclusion of all students. In A. Anderson (Ed.), *Mainstreaming digest* (pp. 109–113). College Park, MD: University of Maryland Press.

MacDonald, S. (1997). *The portfolio and its use: A road map for assessment.* Little Rock, AR: Southern Early Childhood Association.

Maggi, A. (1999). Poetic stones: Roslin Chapel in Gandy's sketchbook and Daguerre's diorama. *Architectural History, 42,* 263–283.

Mandernach, B. J. (2003a). *Developing essay items.* [Online article]. Retrieved July 7, 2006, from www.park.edu/cetl/quicktips/essay.html

Mandernach, B. J. (2003b). *Developing short answer items.* [Online article]. Retrieved July 7, 2006, from www.park.edu/cetl/quicktips/shortanswer.html

Mandernach, B. J. (2003c). *Effective multiple-choice items.* [Online article]. Retrieved July 7, 2006, from www.park.edu/cetl/quicktips/multiple.html

Mandernach, B. J. (2003d). *Quality true–false items.* [Online article]. Retrieved July 7, 2006, from www.park.edu/cetl/quicktips/truefalse.html

Manzo, A. (1969). ReQuest: A method for improving reading comprehension through reciprocal questioning. *Journal of Reading, 12,* 123–126.

Marshall, J. (1974). *George and Martha.* New York: Houghton Mifflin.

Mastropieri, M. A., Scruggs, T. E., & Graetz, J. E. (2003). Reading comprehension instruction for secondary students: Challenges for struggling students and teachers. *Learning Disability Quarterly, 26,* 103–116.

Mayer, R. E., & Gallini, J. K. (1990). When is an illustration worth ten thousand words? *Journal of Educational Psychology, 82,* 715–726.

McCarrier, A., Pinnell, G. S., & Fountas, I. C. (2000). *Interactive writing: How language and literacy come together, K–2.* Portsmouth, NH: Heinemann.

McCullen, C. (1997). Evaluating student presentations. Information Technology Evaluation Services, North Carolina Department of Public Instruction. Retrieved February 7, 2007, from www.ncsu.edu/midlink/rub.pres.html

McKenna, M. C., & Robinson, R. D. (1980). *An introduction to the Cloze procedure: An annotated bibliography.* Newark, DE: International Reading Association.

McTighe, J., & Wiggins, G. (2013). *Essential questions: Opening doors to student learning.* Alexandria, VA: ASCD.

Meyer, D. K., Turner, J. C., & Spencer, C. A. (1997). Challenge in a mathematics classroom: Students' motivation and strategies in project-based learning. *The Elementary School Journal, 97,* 501–521.

Michaels, S., O'Connor, M. C., Hall, M. W., & Resnick, L. B. (2010). *Accountable Talk® sourcebook: For classroom conversation that works* (v.3.1). University of Pittsburgh Institute for Learning. Retrieved from http://ifl.lrdc.pitt.edu

Moore, D. W., & Readence, J. E. (1984). A quantitative and qualitative review of graphic organizer research. *Journal of Educational Research, 78,* 11–17.

Morris, W. (1995). *My dog Skip.* New York: Random House.

National Research Council. (2000). *How people learn: Brain, mind, experience, and school.* J. D. Bransford, A. L. Brown, & R. R. Cocking (Eds.). Commission on Behavioral and Social Sciences and Education. Washington, DC: National Academy Press.

National Staff Development Council. (2001). *Standards for staff development* (Rev. ed.). Oxford, OH: Author.

Naylor, P. R. (1991). *Shiloh.* New York: Atheneum.

New Standards. (2001). *Speaking and listening for preschool through third grade.* Washington, DC: Author.

Ong, W. J. (1991). *Orality and literacy: The technologizing of the word.* New York: Routledge.

Orenstein, P. (1994). *Schoolgirls: Young women, self-esteem, and the confidence gap.* New York: Doubleday.

Ouaknin, M. A. (1999). *Mysteries of the alphabet: The origins of writing.* New York: Abbeville Press.

Oxley, D. (2005). *Smaller learning communities: Implementing and deepening practice.* Portland, OR: Northwest Regional Educational Laboratory.

Palacio, R.J. (2012). *Wonder.* New York: Alfred A. Knopf.

Paratore, J. R., & Robertson, D. A. (2013). *Talk that teaches: Using strategic talk to help students achieve the Common Core.* New York: Guilford Press.

Park, L. S. (2005). *Project Mulberry.* New York: Clarion.

Pearson, P. D., & Gallagher, G. (1983). The gradual release of responsibility model of instruction. *Contemporary Educational Psychology, 8,* 112–123.

Phelan, R. (July 10, 2013). Transition to SBAC: Checklist for school leaders. Sonoma County Office of Education website. Retrieved at http://www.scoe.org/pub/htdocs/blog-tech.html?id=69#.UqTwVWRDvDN

Podlozny, A. (2000). Strengthening verbal skills through the use of classroom drama: A clear link. *Journal of Aesthetic Education, 34*(3/4), 239–275.

Popham, W. J. (2003). Living (or dying) with your NCLB tests. *School Administrator, 60*(11), 10–14.

Radmacher, S. A., & Latosi-Sawin, E. (1995). Summary writing: A tool to improve student comprehension and writing in psychology. *Teaching of Psychology, 22,* 113–115.

Raphael, T. E., Highfield, K., & Au, K. H. (2006). *QAR now: Question answer relationships.* New York: Scholastic.

Rawls, W. (1961).*Where the red fern grows: The story of two dogs and a boy.* Garden City: Doubleday.

Resnick, L. B. (2000). Making America smarter. *Education Week, 18*(40), 38–40.

Ringgold, F. (1992). *Aunt Harriet's Underground Railroad in the sky.* New York: Crown.

Ritchie, D., & Karge, B. D. (1996). Making information memorable: Enhanced knowledge retention and recall through the elaboration process. *Preventing School Failure, 41*(1), 28–33.

Roediger III, H. L., Putnam, A. L., & Smith, M. A. (2011). Ten benefits of testing and their applications to educational practice. *Psychology of Learning & Motivation,* (55), 1–36.

Rowe, M. B. (1986). Wait-time: Slowing down may be a way of speeding up. *Journal of Teacher Education, 37*(1), 43–50.

Royer, R., & Royer, J. (2004). Comparing hand drawn and computer generated concept mapping. *Journal of Computers in Mathematics and Science Teaching, 23*(1), 67–81.

Sadker, D., & Zittleman, K.R. (2009). *Still failing at fairness: How gender bias cheats girls and boys in school and what we can do about it.* New York: Scribner.

Sadker, M., & Sadker, D. (1995). *Failing at fairness: How America's schools cheat girls.* New York: C. Scribner.

Santa, C., & Havens, L. (1995). *Creating independence through student-owned strategies: Project CRISS.* Dubuque, IA: Kendall-Hunt.

Schauble, L. (1996). The development of scientific reasoning in knowledge-rich contexts. *Developmental Psychology, 32,* 102–119.

Schmoker, M. (2006). *Results now: How we can achieve unprecedented improvements in teaching and learning.* Alexandria, VA: ASCD.

Schroeder, A. (1996). *Minty: A story of young Harriet Tubman.* New York: Dial Books for Young Readers.

Shanahan, T., & Shanahan, C. (2008). Teaching disciplinary literacy to adolescents: Rethinking content-area literacy. *Harvard Educational Review, 78,* 40–59.

Shanker, J. L., & Ekwall, E. E. (2003). *Locating and correcting reading difficulties* (8th ed.). Upper Saddle River, NJ: Merrill/Prentice Hall.

Shaughnessy, J. M. (1977). Misconceptions of probability: An experiment with a small-group, activity-based, model building approach to introductory probability at the college level. *Educational Studies in Mathematics, 8,* 295–316.

Shetterly, R. (2005). *Americans who tell the truth.* New York: Dutton Children's Books.

Skillings, M. J., & Ferrell, R. (2000). Student-generated rubrics: Bringing students into the assessment process. *The Reading Teacher, 53,* 452–455.

Slama, R. B. (2011). A longitudinal analysis of academic English proficiency outcomes for adolescent English language learners in the United States. *Journal of Educational Psychology, 104*(2), 265–285.

Smith, R. C. (1920). Popular misconceptions in natural history. *Scientific Monthly, 10*(2), 163–169.

Stein, R. C. (1997). *The Underground Railroad.* New York: Children's Press.

Stipek, D. (2004). Teaching practices in kindergarten and first grade: Different strokes for different folks. *Early Childhood Research Quarterly, 19,* 548–568.

Strickland, D., & Riley-Ayers, S. (2006). *Early literacy: Policy and practice in the preschool years.* New Brunswick: NJ: National Institute for Early Education Research.

Summers, J. J. (2006). Effects of collaborative learning in math on sixth graders' individual goal orientations from a socioconstructivist perspective. *Elementary School Journal, 106,* 273–290.

Terman, L. M. (1916). *The measurement of intelligence: An explanation of and a complete guide for the use of the Standard revision and extension of the Binet-Simon intelligence scale.* Boston: Houghton Mifflin.

Tierney, R. J. (1998). Literacy assessment reform: Shifting beliefs, principled possibilities, and emerging practices. *The Reading Teacher, 51,* 374–390.

Tomlinson, C. A. (1999). *The differentiated classroom: Responding to the needs of all learners.* Alexandria, VA: ASCD.

Tuckman, B. W. (1998). Using tests as an incentive to motivate procrastinators to study. *Journal of Experimental Education, 66*(2), 141–147.

Vosniadou, S., Ioannides, C., Dimitrakopoulou, A., & Papademetriou, E. (2001). Designing learning environments to promote conceptual change in science. *Learning and Instruction, 11,* 381–419.

Walsh, J. A., & Sattes, B. D. (2011). *Thinking through quality questioning: Deepening student engagement.* Thousand Oaks, CA: Corwin.

Wang, C. (2000). How to grade essay examinations. *Performance Improvement, 39*(1), 12–15.

Webb, L. D. (2006). *The history of American education: A great American experiment.* Upper Saddle River, NJ: Pearson/Merrill/Prentice Hall.

Webb, N. L. (2007). Issues related to judging the alignment of curriculum standards and assessments. *Applied Measurement In Education, 20*(1), 7–25.

White, J., & Gardner, J. (2011). *The classroom x-factor: The power of body language and non-verbal communication in teaching.* New York: Routledge.

Wiggins, G. P., & McTighe, J. (1998). *Understanding by design.* Alexandria, VA: ASCD.

Wiggins, G. P., & McTighe, J. (2005). *Understanding by design* (Expanded 2nd ed.). Alexandria, VA: ASCD.

Wiggins, G. & McTighe, J. (2013). *Essential Questions: Opening Doors to Student Understanding.* Alexandria, VA: ASCD

Wilcox, B. L. (1997). Writing portfolios: Active vs. passive. *English Journal, 86,* 34–37.

Wilde, O. (1891/1993). *The picture of Dorian Grey.* New York: Dover.

Winerip, M. (2005, May 4). SAT essay test rewards length and ignores errors. *New York Times.* Retrieved July 6, 2006, from www.freerepublic.com/focus/f-news/1397024/posts

Winter, J. (1988). *Follow the drinking gourd.* New York: Knopf.

Wolf, D. (1987). Child development and different cognitive styles. *In Seminar proceedings: Issues in discipline-based art education: Strengthening the stage, extending the horizons* (pp. 3–8). Los Angeles: Getty Center for Education in the Arts.

Wong, H. K., & Wong, R. T. (2005). *First days of school: How to be an effective teacher.* Mountain View, CA: Author.

Wood, D., Bruner, J. S., & Ross, G. (1976). The role of tutoring in problem solving. *Journal of Psychology and Psychiatry, 17*(2), 89–100.

Wright, C. C. (1994). *Journey to freedom: A story of the Underground Railroad.* New York: Holiday House.

Yeh, S. S. (2005). Limiting the unintended consequences of high-stakes testing. *Education Policy Analysis Archives, 13*(43), 1–23.

Zike, D. (1992). *Dinah Zike's big book of books and activities: An illustrated guide for teachers, parents, and anyone who works with kids!* San Antonio, TX: Dinah-Might Adventures.

Zike, D. (2004). *Dinah Zike's big book of science: Elementary K–6.* San Antonio, TX: Dinah-Might Adventures.

Index

The Letter *f* following a page number denotes a figure.

About the Authors

Douglas Fisher, PhD, is a professor of language and literacy education in the Department of Teacher Education at San Diego State University (SDSU), the codirector for the Center for the Advancement of Reading at the California State University Chancellor's Office, and a past director of professional development for the City Heights Educational Collaborative. He is the recipient of the International Reading Association Celebrate Literacy Award as well as the Christa McAuliffe award for excellence in teacher education from the American Association of State Colleges and Universities. He has published numerous articles on reading and literacy, differentiated instruction, and curriculum design as well as books, including *Creating Literacy-Rich Schools for Adolescents* (with Gay Ivey), *Improving Adolescent Literacy: Strategies at Work* (with Nancy Frey), and *Teaching English Language Learners: A Differentiated Approach* (with Carol Rothenberg). Doug has taught a variety of courses in SDSU's teacher-credentialing program as well as graduate-level courses on English language development and literacy. A former early intervention specialist and language development specialist, he has also taught high school English, writing, and literacy development to public school students. He can be reached at dfisher@mail.sdsu.edu.

Nancy Frey, PhD, is an associate professor of literacy in the School of Teacher Education at San Diego State University. Before joining the university faculty, Nancy was a teacher in the Broward County (Florida) Public Schools, where she taught both general and special education students at the elementary and middle school levels. She later worked for the Florida Department of Education on a statewide project for supporting students with diverse learning needs in general education curriculum. She is also a recipient of the Christa McAuliffe award for excellence in teacher education. Her research interests include reading and literacy, assessment, intervention, and curriculum design. She has coauthored several books on literacy, including *Language Arts Workshop: Purposeful Reading and Writing Instruction* and *Reading for Information in Elementary School* (both with Doug Fisher). She teaches a variety of courses in SDSU's teacher-credentialing program on elementary and secondary literacy in content-area instruction and supporting students with diverse learning needs. She can be reached at nfrey@mail.sdsu.edu.

WANT TO
Learn More?

ASCD is a worldwide learning community of teachers, principals, superintendents, curriculum developers, and other instructional leaders. This ever-growing organization is dedicated to learning and teaching and the success of each student.

Members receive the award-winning magazine *Educational Leadership* and many other valuable benefits, including books like the one you're reading now.

Memberships are available from as low as US$29.

Join ASCD Today!

To learn more, go to **www.ascd.org/learnmore** or call (toll-free in the United States and Canada) 1-800-933-ASCD (2723) or 1-703-578-9600.

LEARN. TEACH. LEAD.

1703 North Beauregard Street
Alexandria, VA 22311-1714 USA

www.ascd.org/learnmore